DEVELOPING
A DYNAMIC
MISSION FOR
YOUR MINISTRY

Other Books by Aubrey Malphurs
Biblical Manhood and Womanhood
Ministry Nuts and Bolts
Strategy 2000

DEVELOPING A DYNAMIC MISSION FOR YOUR MINISTRY

Aubrey Malphurs

krēgel
PUBLICATIONS

Grand Rapids, MI 49501

Developing a Dynamic Mission for Your Ministry: Finding Direction and Making an Impact As a Church Leader

Copyright © 1998 by Aubrey Malphurs

Published by Kregel Publications, a division of Kregel, Inc., P.O. Box 2607, Grand Rapids, MI 49501. Kregel Publications provides trusted, biblical publications for Christian growth and service. Your comments and suggestions are valued.

For more information about Kregel Publications, visit our web site at www.kregel.com.

Cover design: Alan G. Hartman
Book design: Nicholas G. Richardson

Library of Congress Cataloging-in-Publication Data
Malphurs, Aubrey.
    Developing a dynamic mission for your ministry: finding direction and making an impact as a church leader / Aubrey Malphurs.
        p.   cm.
    1. Mission of the church. I. Title.
BV601.8.M32   1998   253—dc21   98-10292
                                                                        CIP
ISBN 0-8254-3189-1

Printed in the United States of America

1 2 3 / 04 03 02 01 00 99 98

Contents

96756

Introduction

   Pastor Larry Brown walked out of the mission seminar with ideas brightly popping in his head like the multicolored
fireworks on the fourth of July. He had reluctantly mailed in the $150
reservation fee for Faith Community Church's Conference for Leaders. He had attended several church leadership conferences in his
area and the central message was beginning to sound repetitive: vision, vision, vision! While he recognized that a clear, challenging
vision was vital to his ministry and his church, he wasn't sure that
he understood the concept. Someone at one conference said that a
vision was more caught than taught, and he believed that he simply hadn't caught it—at least not yet. Consequently, as various well-
known leaders emphasized the need for a compelling, God-glorifying
vision, he felt a sense of despair slowly creeping into his life.
   However, this seminar on mission was a real eye-opener. It seemed
that in his reading—he was a voracious reader—he had come across
an occasional article on mission, but each was buried under numerous articles on vision. For him the concept of mission seemed just as
important as that of vision and was a lot easier to comprehend. A
strong sense of mission as well as a vision was what his church
needed. The leader of the seminar—a seminary professor—had provided him and the others present with enough information to discover and develop a fully functional mission statement for their
churches. This was critical because it filled Pastor Brown with hope
for his struggling ministry. He knew that a unique vision was important to his church as well, but that would come later. For the
present his goal was to develop a positive direction that would signal to his people where they were going.

Pastor Larry Brown was surprised that a seminary professor had led the seminar. He had attended a large, well-known evangelical seminary where no one had ever said much of anything about the need for a vision statement much less a mission statement. Instead, he had received much training in the Scriptures, the original languages, and theology, for which he was grateful. However, when he became pastor of Grace Community Church, he found that he was totally unprepared to lead the church. That the church consisted of around 120 people and was in serious decline did not help the situation either. Based on the mission seminar, he quickly realized that his church had no sense of direction. Neither he nor his congregation had ever asked, Where are we going? or Where should we be going? However, that was soon to change.

▼▼▼

When I wrote my first book on vision in 1992, there was little available on the topic and virtually no one was talking about it in the ministry world. I expected that other books devoted exclusively to the topic would follow. Though surprisingly few have been written exclusively on the concept, vision has become a ministry buzzword. Everyone is using it! If you, like me, are on several large church's mailing lists, especially those that sponsor a leadership or pastor's conference, the term *vision* virtually screams at you in almost every mailer. Today, if I read a book in the areas of leadership and church growth and the author doesn't use the V-word or mention the concept, I'm surprised. I'm left wondering if the author has made the transition into the twentieth century.

I have written on the concepts of ministry vision, core values, and strategy.[1] I am convinced that all are vital concepts for those who would have a significant ministry impact on our world in the twenty-first century. However, another vital concept that far too many have overlooked is a ministry mission. The topic isn't exactly a new one. In researching material for this book, I have discovered a number of authors in the marketplace who make at least some passing reference to it. In *The 7 Habits of Highly Effective People*, Stephen Covey writes, "One of the most important thrusts of my work with organizations is to assist them in developing effective mission statements."[2] In a discussion of the qualities of a leader, Peter Drucker writes: "What matters is not the leader's charisma. What matters is the leader's mission. Therefore, the first job of the leader is to think through and define the mission of the institution."[3] In my role as a trainer with churches and denominations, I am convinced that a dynamic ministry mission is as important, if not in some cases more important, as a clear, challenging vision, especially for all those leaders who struggle with the envisioning process. Indeed, the act of leadership is fundamentally the act of articulating first a ministry mission statement and then pursuing it.

I have stated that the ministry mission concept has been virtually overlooked. The problem is threefold. First, like Grace Community Church, very few churches have articulated a clear, compelling mission for their ministry. Many of these are North American churches that are small and struggling for survival at the end of the second and the beginning of the third millennium. In *The New Reformation*, Lyle Schaller writes that ". . . 50 percent of all Protestant congregations averaged 85 or fewer at worship in 1995."[4] Also, as many as 80 to 85 percent of America's churches have plateaued or are in decline.

A major characteristic of these small, struggling churches is that they focus more on being than doing. Being has everything to do with survival; doing has more to do with success. Churches that concentrate their energy on being tend not to think much about doing, and it's the latter that emphasizes such things as mission, vision, values, and other vital concepts.

Second, there is a dearth of Christian material on mission. Few Christians are writing on the topic. While some in the marketplace such as Covey and Drucker address the importance of mission, it's only one of many topics they cover in their writings. And fewer still discuss how to develop and write a mission statement for one's business or ministry.

Third, I have observed much confusion over the concepts of mission, vision, and values. I'm convinced that many who use the term *vision* are, in fact, talking about mission. An article entitled "A Variety of Visions" that appeared in *Leadership* presented eleven vision statements from various congregations across the nation.[5] According to my understanding, only one or maybe two were actual vision statements, the rest were mission statements some of which were combined with a statement of strategy. In *Say It & Live It*, Jones and Kahaner also acknowledge that "corporations have used the term 'mission statement' to include all kinds of philosophical statements, including mission, values, visions, principles, credos, bonds, and so on."[6] I would argue that values, mission, vision, and strategy are so important that every ministry should develop and articulate each as separate from the other. Consequently, in training leaders, I have them write out individual statements for each. Therefore, the purpose of this book is to help you as leaders develop and articulate a definitive, well-thought-out mission statement for your ministry.

In this book, I will quote occasionally from secular writings on the topic of mission. I believe that all truth is God's truth, but not all of God's truth is contained within the pages of Scripture. While all that the Bible says is true (John 17:17; 2 Tim. 2:15), there are divine truths that God chose not to include in his Word. Had he done this, the Bible would be a massive, cumbersome book. I believe that some secular sources have unknowingly tapped into God's truth. That is why some of what they say is true, especially in the area of leadership. Since Moses listened to the advice of his father-in-law, Jethro, who may have been an unbeliever (Exod. 18), I listen to what secular writers say about leadership topics such as mission. However, I'm careful to pass what they say through a theological filter. Consequently, I view these secular writings as my "Jethros."

Developing a Dynamic Mission for Your Ministry consists of eight chapters. Chapter 1 emphasizes the importance of the mission statement and supplies nine reasons why every ministry should have one. Chapter 2 defines precisely what a mission is so that leaders don't fall into the trap of confusing it with other vital ministry concepts. Chapter 3 continues the discussion of definition but emphasizes the distinctions between two commonly confused concepts—mission and vision. Chapter 4 begins with instruction on how to develop a mission statement for your ministry. The process consists of the four *ps*. This chapter covers the first three: the preparation, personnel, and process of mission development. Under the latter, I provide four steps that help you craft a mission statement tailor-made for your ministry. Chapter 5 is also about developing the mission and adds the final *p*—the product—the mission statement itself. Here you test your mission statement to see if it's a good one. However, if no one knows or understands your mission, then you might as well not have one. Thus, chapter 6 presents nine ways to communicate your mission to your ministry constituency. Chapter 7 helps leaders implement their mission through a carefully refined ministry strategy. Chapter 8 provides insight on how your ministry can preserve its mission, despite the influx of institutional dry rot.

Finally, this book is all about the ministry basics. If mission doesn't represent the *a*, then for sure it's the *b* of the ministry ABCs (the *a* is core values, and the *c* is vision). However, in taking you back to the basics—the very foundational concepts for ministry—don't be surprised to find yourself at the ministry cutting edge. In many ways, you'll be traveling like pioneers through uncharted territory. So prepare yourself for a trip that will not only inform and train you, but will challenge you for high-impact ministry in the twenty-first century.

ENDNOTES

1. Aubrey Malphurs, *Developing a Vision for Ministry in the 21st Century* (Grand Rapids: Baker Book House, 1992). Aubrey Malphurs, *Values-Driven Leadership* (Grand Rapids: Baker Book House, 1996). Aubrey Malphurs, *Strategy 2000* (Grand Rapids: Kregel Publications, 1996).

2. Stephen R. Covey, *The 7 Habits of Highly Effective People* (New York: Simon & Shuster, 1989), 139.

3. Peter F. Drucker, *Managing the Non-Profit Organization* (New York: Harper Business, 1990), 3.

4. Lyle E. Schaller, *The New Reformation* (Nashville: Abingdon Press, 1995), 43.

5. Mary Ann Jeffries, "A Variety of Visions," *Leadership* 15, no. 3 (Summer 1994): 35.

6. Patricia Jones and Larry Kahaner, *Say It & Live It* (New York: Doubleday, 1995), 263.

1

The Importance of the Mission

Nine Reasons Why a Mission Is Important

Pastor Larry Brown left the leadership conference convinced that he had to develop a dynamic mission for his church. What made that conference worth the $150 fee? For one thing, the seminary professor who taught the seminar began with nine reasons why a mission was critical to the life of a church or parachurch ministry. For Pastor Brown that list supplied a major missing piece to his ministry puzzle.

Actually, numerous reasons exist why a mission is important to a ministry. There is no complete list for any of the vital ministry concepts. However, the seminar supplied nine major ones that grabbed and held Pastor Larry's attention. This chapter will provide you with all nine reasons and save you the cost and time of attending a leadership conference.

1. THE MISSION DETERMINES THE MINISTRY'S DIRECTION

It's reported that Peter Drucker said, "If you don't know where you're going, any plan will do." It's also rumored that former New York Yankee catcher Yogi Berra once uttered, "If you don't know where you're going, you might end up somewhere else." In their own inimitable ways, both men are stressing the profound importance of having a direction in life. This is true not only for an individual but for an institution, whether it's the church or the parachurch.

If you desire to be a leader, it's essential that you know where you're going. A successful leader is a successful direction setter, and the key to the leader's direction is his or her mission. When all is said and done, it's the ministry's mission that determines the ministry's direction. The act of leadership is fundamentally the act of articulating a dynamic, core mission and then pursuing it. And it's the mission that provides the target toward which the ministry takes aim. A clear understanding of mission helps an organization answer the *direction* question: Where are we going? or Where do we want to go? If you don't know where you're going, then Yogi is correct, "You might end up somewhere else." However, another possibility is that you might end up nowhere.

▼▼▼

If you desire to be a leader, it's essential that you know where you're going.

▲▲▲

Leaders in the Bible demonstrated a strong sense of mission. Moses, once on track, pursued with a passion his mission to lead Israel out of Egyptian bondage (Exod. 3:10). The same is true of Joshua, Daniel, and Nehemiah. The Savior's ministry was directed by his mission (Mark 10:45), and Paul evidenced a passionate direction throughout his entire ministry (Rom. 15:20). I'll say more about these and others when I define mission in chapter 2.

I believe that a major reason why 80 to 85 percent of the churches in America are in trouble is because they don't have a clear, compelling mission—they don't know where they're going or should be going. Either they've not asked the direction question, or they've asked it but not been able to answer it. Not to have a mission is not to have a direction or a target in life. For some this represents safety. It reminds me of the person who shoots the proverbial arrow at the wall, grabs a can of paint, runs up to the wall, and paints a bull's-eye around the embedded arrow. Not having a mission makes failure a lot easier to swallow—who can say you missed the mark? However, not having a mission in many ways ensures ministry failure.

A well-focused mission statement provides a target on the wall for the archer and all else who might launch the ministry arrow. It says to everyone that this is where we're going. A clear, dynamic mission serves a number of purposes. First, it helps people outside the ministry determine if they want to be a part of the ministry. If a church, for example, is moving in a different direction than a potential member or future staff person, then there is no mission match. It would be a mistake for the individual to become a part of the ministry. Both would be pulling in different directions, and, in time, they would pull apart.

Second, by painting a clear, well-defined target on the wall, everyone who is a part of the ministry organization knows where to direct their energies. The mission focuses people's energy on what they're attempting to accomplish. The absence of a mission, however, disperses the ministry's energy in numerous different directions and accomplishes little. Over time, people wise up to what is happening and put forth less and less energy. The result is a maintenance ministry where all expend just enough energy to keep the ministry alive.

Finally, the ministry that has a clear direction is likely to be significantly more effective because it begins with its end in mind. It's not simply shooting in the dark. It knows what it wants to accomplish and there's little reason not to pursue the same.

2. THE MISSION FORMULATES THE MINISTRY'S FUNCTION

Along with its direction, the mission helps a ministry formulate or precisely determine its biblical task. It answers the *function* question: What are we supposed to be doing? What function does the organization exist to perform? What is the primary thing that God has called us to accomplish? What are we attempting to do for him and our people? It's an expression of intent. It summarizes and presents the church's primary biblical task. It determines the results that it seeks to obtain.

Note carefully that the function question isn't, What *are* we doing? Although that is an important question that leaders must ask, especially as they regularly plan and evaluate, it's not the key to formulating the ministry's function. Every ministry is doing something whether good, bad, or a combination thereof. The function question is, What *should* we be doing? That is a sobering question for any church or leadership team. It gets their attention; it causes them to stop and think theologically not only about what they're doing, but what they should be doing. It's also a dangerous question because it may surface the different agendas that people may have for a ministry's purpose.

The function question is a basic question for every ministry. It's foundational. It's part of the ministry ABCs and all ministries should be asking it periodically throughout their existence. When asked, it has a way of keeping a ministry on target. However, as I work with churches and various denominations, I find that most have not and are not asking the function question. This means that many don't know what they're doing or what they are supposed to be doing. The one exception is those who have invested their lives into church planting. To some degree they're forced to deal with their primary task. One of my functions at Dallas Seminary is to train church plant-ers. I make sure that they all have asked and answered the function question for their prospective church plants because some may miss it in the planting process.

▼▼▼

The function question is a basic question
for every ministry. It's foundational.
It's part of the ministry ABCs.

▲▲▲

In working with established churches, most of which range in size from eighty-five to two hundred people, I find that few can clearly answer the function question. If someone has asked it in the past or at the founding of the ministry, it has long since been forgotten. The function question generates much discussion and surfaces various opinions about what the function of the church should be. It's sur-prising to listen to a board of laymen discuss the biblical function of the church. Many don't have a clue. It's even more surprising and alarming when the pastor, or in some cases the pastoral staff, often seminary graduates, can add little to the discussion.

It's my opinion that not understanding the primary task or func-tion is a major reason why so many churches are plateaued or in decline now at the end of the twentieth century. Some simply don't know where they're going. Some are moving in several different di-rections at the same time. Others are moving in a single direction, but it's the wrong direction. An example is the church who views its sole function as evangelism, or the church that sees its only purpose as teaching. When I meet with them and ask the basic function question, most are puzzled and struggle to come up with a clear answer. This is because the biblical function of many of these churches has long since been lost. Somewhere along the way, they've become so busy doing ministry that they've not taken the time to think about the ministry they should be doing.

There are several advantages for having a mission that formu-lates a ministry's function. One is that the mission serves to posi-tion the organization in the Christian and non-Christian community. People know what the church stands for. Another is that it infuses the ministry with meaning. It says that what we're doing is important and has value. A third is that a truly biblical mission forces the church to look outward at the church's neigh-boring community as well as inward at its believing community.

A fourth is that it determines how the ministry can make a difference in its community.

3. THE MISSION FOCUSES THE MINISTRY'S FUTURE

We've learned that every ministry must ask and answer two questions. One is the *direction* question: Where are we going? And the second is the *function* question: What are we supposed to be doing? Both address a ministry's future. That's because mission, like vision, has everything to do with the future. A clear, biblical mission serves to bring into focus the church or parachurch ministry's future.

In Philippians 3:13–14, Paul writes: "Brothers, I do not consider myself yet to have taken hold of it. But one thing I do: Forgetting what is behind and straining toward what is ahead, I press on toward the goal to win the prize for which God has called me heavenward in Christ Jesus." Essentially, Paul is saying that we must look to the future, not live in the past. I believe that the biblical perspective is to learn from our past—both the good and the bad—but not to live in that past. Living in the past while trying to move forward is contradictory if not impossible. It's similar to driving a car forward while looking through the rearview mirror. It's difficult at best and dangerous for sure. Yet it's imperative that a ministry move toward the future.

But how can your ministry know the future? Outside of biblical prophecy, can anyone know what the future holds? The correct answer is that you can't predict the future, but you can predetermine your ministry's future. Someone has said that the best way to predict the future is to create it. And the way to create your ministry's future is to develop a dynamic, biblical ministry mission. It's the mission formulation that defines the church or parachurch's desired or preferred future state.

▼▼▼

The best way to predict the future is to create it.

▲▲▲

What leaders must understand is that a ministry itself must invent its own future or someone or something else will. When a ship leaves its port, it knows where it's going and thus can predict its future. However, if the engine malfunctions, then the ship may not reach its destination. At that point, the ship is most vulnerable and ceases to determine its future. Instead, the winds and the tides move the ship in various directions, which will result in the ultimate demise of the vessel. A ministry without a mission is much like that crippled ship. If the ministry doesn't define its future, then a power-ful person in the congregation, a city council, the federal govern-ment, even Satan, sits in the ministry driving seat.

An effective statement of mission describes not only what the or-ganization is but also what it wants to become in a way that sets high aspirations. By pointing everyone toward its preferred future, it calls upon everyone's God-given creative reserves. It reinforces the belief that all are engaged in the critical process of creating the min-istry organization. People engaged in inventing and drafting the mission need to know their ministry not only as it exists in the present but as it must exist in the future. What *is*, is important, but what *can be* is even more important.

4. THE MISSION PROVIDES A TEMPLATE FOR DECISION MAKING

A dynamic mission not only focuses the ministry's future, it sets important boundaries. It determines what the church or parachurch organization will and will not attempt to do; it helps it to say yes to some things and no to others. Mission is to the ministry what a com-pass is to an explorer, a map to a tourist, a rudder to a ship, a tem-plate to a machinist. It provides a framework for thinking; it's the standard or criterion that guides all decision making. On the one hand, it transcends today; on the other, it guides and informs to-day. If a church's mission is disciple making (Matt. 28:19–20), then everything it does must contribute in some significant way to the making of disciples. If it doesn't, then you don't do it.

Every ministry will experience difficult, trying times—it comes with the spiritual territory. Churches can rely on their mission statements to help them through these complex times when they have to make tough decisions. There will be little need to have long, possibly divi-sive discussions about how the ministry will handle each situation. The mission statement should tell you what decisions to make and how to act. The first thing to decide is, What is our mission? or What are we supposed to be doing? The second decision is, Does this (new program, ministry, etc.) enhance or detract from our mission?

▼▼▼

*The mission is the standard that
guides all decision making.*

▲▲▲

A clear, well-defined mission protects both a pastor and the church from getting involved in all kinds of tangential activities. You'll discover this when sincere, well-meaning people—even members of the board—suggest that the pastor or the church pursue this or that. They do this because certain people have their own agendas for the church and its leader. Regardless, there are numerous good activities and events that could be an important part of your church's ministry. However, you don't have the time or the people to do them all, nor does God expect you to. Churches or leaders that attempt too many activities usually wind up doing them poorly, if at all. You must determine how a particular activity or program squares with your mission statement. If a certain congregant questions your lack of involvement in a particular program or committee that you believe is not justified, then you point him or her to the mission statement.

The mission serves as a guide not only for major activities and events but for the day-to-day decision making within your organization. It works like a filter to screen out the unessential. There is so much that is happening every day in the average ministry that you can lose yourself in objectives and minutiae that are unrelated or only distantly related to the mission. They become distractions from the principal goal. Anything that doesn't contribute toward the ministry objective, no matter how insignificant, should be filtered out and questioned.

5. THE MISSION INSPIRES MINISTRY UNITY

Scripture is emphatic about the importance of unity among Christians. In his prayer in John 17:20–23, the Savior prays that all believers would be one. The result of our complete unity is that the world will believe that the Father has truly sent the Son.

> My prayer is not for them alone. I pray also for those who will believe in me through their message, that all of them may be one, Father, just as you are in me and I am in you. May they also be in us so that the world may believe that you have sent me. I have given them the glory that you gave me, that they may be one as we are one: I in them and you in me. May they be brought to complete unity to let the world know that you sent me . . .

Paul also stresses the importance of the unity of Christians within the local church. In Ephesians 4:3, he exhorts those in the church at Ephesus and subsequently all believers to do whatever it takes to maintain unity: "Make every effort to keep the unity of the Spirit through the bond of peace." He follows his exhortation in verses 4–6 with an appeal to the seven elements of unity: "There is one body and one Spirit—just as you were called to one hope when you were called—one Lord, one faith, one baptism; one God and Father of all, who is over all and through all and in all."

One key ingredient that strongly encourages unity is a dynamic, compelling mission statement. Clarifying your ministry mission will eliminate a great deal of unnecessary conflict in your work and will help direct all discussion and activity productively. A clear direction provides a unifying theme for the organization's members, and draws them together as a team or a community. It defines the arenas within which it will minister, and charts the future course. This results in a sense of teamwork that adds to the church or parachurch's ministry momentum. Indeed, it's doubtful that any organization will ever achieve excellence for Christ without a basic consensus among its leaders and members on its preferred future.

▼▼▼

A clear direction provides a unifying theme for the organization's members, and draws them together as a team or a community.

▲▲▲

A ministry with no single, consensual mission statement will end up splintered. When a congregation moves in different directions, it loses the focus and momentum that a single direction provides. Ultimately, it doesn't accomplish very much for Christ. One of the reasons why the parachurch movement flourished from the 1960s through the early 1980s is that it locked onto a single mission such as evangelism, discipleship, and so on. One reason why the church hasn't flourished is the lack of a clear, strategic direction. No one knows or understands what they are supposed to be doing. They don't know what to believe in, so people drift away from churches toward organizations that have a clear belief system and direction, such as the parachurch.

Make sure that people understand and agree with your mission as well as your core values and strategy before they become a part of your ministry. Every church has its own unique culture, and those who move to your church will bring much cultural baggage, both good and bad, that they've collected over the years from their former churches. If they join your church and don't agree with the church's mission, then you are guaranteed conflict.

Smaller churches tend to ignore this advice to their peril. Because they need members to survive, they may look the other way when a potential member disagrees with their direction or core values. What they must understand is that these people will exert a greater influence in a small church than in a larger church. Why invite trouble to begin with? When those who desire to become a part of your ministry disagree with your direction, then you do them and yourself a service by pointing them toward another ministry that is moving in their direction.

6. THE MISSION WELCOMES HELPFUL CHANGE

Holding to a compelling sense of direction for your ministry isn't always easy. One reason is that everything in and around the organization is changing at breakneck speed. The fact is that we're living in an era of unprecedented change much like that of the early church. Like a performer balanced on a tight rope, all of Western civilization is precariously balanced between two eras. Futurist Alvin Toffler has labeled this period from 1950 to 2020 a "hinge of history," during which a major paradigm shift is occurring as a new order breaks away from the old, and society moves into a new epoch. Others describe the period as a "whitewater age" in which those who aren't prepared will find themselves dashed against the rocks of destruction.

These can prove to be times of great challenge and opportunity as well as dangerous times for the ministry. While many churches believe that all change is bad, nothing could be further from the truth. Some changes are good for a ministry and others are bad; some will help your church while others can hurt it. The key to success is the choices an institution and its leaders make. It must be able to quickly analyze and understand the various changes as they take place, and then determine what will or will not benefit the organization.

How does the leader know which changes will help the ministry and which ones will harm it? How can he or she know what to change and what to leave as is? Again, the key is a clear, decisive mission. The organization that has no direction will not be able to answer these questions and survive. Only the church or parachurch ministry that has a well-thought-through, consensual mission will survive this catastrophic time of intense change. That mission will serve to guide the church or ministry around the treacherous rocks and find the friendly currents that are always present in the whitewater of change. Once they've analyzed and understood the implications of a particular change, leaders must ask: Will this change help us in accomplishing our biblical function or will it hinder us? The mission will serve as the filter through which all change is poured. What you filter out is discarded. What gets through is kept.

▼▼▼

Only the church or parachurch ministry that has a well-thought-through, consensual mission will survive this catastrophic time of intense change.

▲▲▲

A good way to get a head start on how the new technology of the twenty-first century will affect our lives and ministries is to read Bill Gates' book *The Road Ahead.* In this important work, Gates—who built Microsoft into one of the most successful companies in the world—conducts us along the information highway and gives his vision of what he believes the future holds for us. He's convinced that we're on the brink of crossing a technology threshold that will forever change the way we buy, work, learn, and communicate. Just as the personal computer has revolutionized the late twentieth century, so the tools of the information age, which are rapidly becoming a present reality, will transform the way we make choices about almost everything.

The information highway can serve the church to advance the kingdom of God in this world. However, it would be absurd to assume that all this technology is for the good. Problems will surface with the information highway just as they have with the personal computer. How may we as leaders discern the best way to take advantage of new technology? The answer is to travel up and down the highway, not with blinders over our eyes but with a biblical filter in front of our face. That filter is our mission statement, based on the unchanging Word of God.

7. THE MISSION SHAPES A MINISTRY'S STRATEGY

The mission of an organization addresses its future direction and what it's supposed to accomplish. However, it's the organization's strategy that supplies the framework that actually gets it there. While both are mutually dependent, it's the mission that leads and shapes a ministry's strategy. Every strategy must begin with a succinct mission. The mission is always found at the front end of the strategy, and the strategy is only as good as the mission that drives and molds it. Again, if you don't know where you're going, then any road will get you there. The church's mission is the Great Commission mandate in Matthew 28:19–20. The strategy of the early church is found in Acts and includes three missionary journeys that begin in Acts 13.

▼▼▼

The mission is always found at the front end of the strategy, and the strategy is only as good as the mission that drives and molds it.

▲▲▲

Peter Drucker writes: "Strategy determines what the key activities are in a given business. And strategy requires knowing 'what our business is and what it should be.'"[1] The mission defines what our ministry business is and what it should be. It provides the context for the formulation of the strategy. However, a good strategy can't correct a flawed mission. For example, my experience is that a large number of people who serve in churches today, especially people over sixty-five, believe that both the pastor and the church exist to serve and take care of them. While the Reformation corrected a flawed soteriology (salvation by faith), it did little to correct a flawed ecclesiology (the unbiblical idea that the priest or pastor exists to do the work of the ministry). When churches devise their strategies around this unbiblical mission, and many have, they cease to function as a church. Instead, they've become retirement homes and shouldn't call themselves a church.

8. THE MISSION ENHANCES A MINISTRY'S EFFECTIVENESS

I don't know of anyone besides the prophet Jeremiah who began his ministry expecting to fail. Of course this was God's plan, not Jeremiah's. If you investigate the ministries, whether large or small, across North America that have proved effective and are having a powerful impact for the kingdom, you will discover that each has a significant, well-focused mission. All good performance starts with a clear direction. It was true of the early church, and it's true for the church today. Churches that have adopted and truly live out their mission statements are hands-down winners in making a difference for Christ in their communities.

▼▼▼

All good performance starts with a clear direction.

▲▲▲

It comes as no surprise that Peter Drucker has observed much the same in the world of business. He writes the following:

> That business purpose and business mission are so rarely given adequate thought is perhaps the most important single cause of business frustration and business failure. Conversely, in outstanding businesses such as the Telephone Company or Sears, success always rests to a large extent on raising the question "What is our business?" clearly and deliberately, and on answering it thoughtfully and thoroughly.[2]

I suspect that a part of the explanation for this success lies in the fact that the mission expresses the ministry's or business's bottom line—what truly matters—and people are willing to commit themselves to that which matters. This directly affects organizational or congregational integrity—the institution's willingness to live out its mission, even against odds.

If a new church has any hope of being effective spiritually, it must determine its mission right from the start. It's much easier to determine a church's mission at its inception than to wait and attempt it later. However, not everyone is a church planter or involved in starting a new work. Consequently, those who find themselves leading and ministering in a struggling established church should look for the church's mission. Most likely, there will be either no mission or a poorly defined one. The leader's job, then, is to lead the church in developing a well-defined biblical statement.

9. THE MISSION FACILITATES EVALUATION

Over the years, my church planting course at Dallas Seminary has garnered a good reputation among the student body. I am convinced that one reason for this is constant, constructive evaluation by the students who take the course. Because I'm a tenured faculty person, my students are only required to evaluate me once every few years. My personal policy is to ask my students to evaluate me and the course every semester. Why? It's the primary way that I can improve my teaching and the content of the course. I never cease to be amazed at some of the brilliant and creative ideas that students come up with.

I've pastored two churches and served as an interim in numerous others. Yet I don't ever recall anyone ever formally evaluating my leadership or evaluating the church's ministry as an organization. (I don't include in this the occasional beef of an unhappy parishioner, or those who have roast pastor for Sunday lunch.) The church that fails to evaluate its people and its effectiveness as a ministry does itself a great injustice. That which is evaluated not only gets done, but it gets done well. While no person or institution enjoys being under the lens of careful scrutiny, in the long run it serves to improve and fortify.

▼▼▼

That which is evaluated not only gets done, but it gets done well.

▲▲▲

In 2 Corinthians 13:5, Paul instructs the church at Corinth: "Examine yourselves to see whether you are in the faith; test yourselves." Throughout 2 Corinthians, Paul subjected both himself and his ministry to close scrutiny. Now it was time for the Corinthians to do the same—did their lives match up to the faith they professed?

On what basis does one evaluate the church? I would argue that the mission is the standard criterion for that evaluation. When we articulate a compelling, biblical mission, it forces us to hold ourselves accountable for acting and ministering in a way that is congruent with that mission. Once we've created and communicated a mission to our people and the community around our ministry, it becomes a benchmark for evaluating all of our professions and actions. The power of the mission is in the way it forces accountability for all the organization's activities.

SUMMARY

Nine Reasons Why a Mission Is Important
1. It determines the ministry's *direction*.
2. It formulates the ministry's *function*.
3. It focuses the ministry's *future*.
4. It provides a template for *decision making*.
5. It inspires ministry *unity*.
6. It welcomes helpful *change*.
7. It shapes a ministry's *strategy*.
8. It enhances a ministry's *effectiveness*.
9. It facilitates *evaluation*.

QUESTIONS FOR THOUGHT AND DISCUSSION

1. After reading this chapter, are you convinced that your ministry needs a compelling, dynamic mission? Why or why not? Of the nine reasons why a mission is important, which were the most important to you? Why?

2. Does your ministry have a clear direction? Has anyone written that direction down on paper or attempted to communicate it in any way? Do the people who are a part of your ministry know its direction? How many? How do you know?

3. What is your ministry's function, or what is it supposed to be doing? Does the leadership agree on its function? Is it doing what it's supposed to be doing? Explain.

4. What is your ministry's preferred future? Has it attempted to predetermine its future? Why or why not? What are the consequences of not developing a mission that defines the ministry's future?

5. Who makes the decisions that affect your ministry's present and future? How does your ministry make these decisions? Have there been any problems with this process? Explain.

6. Is your ministry characterized by unity? If your answer is yes, is that unity by consensus or compromise? Which would you prefer?

7. Does your ministry have a clear, effective strategy? If yes, do the people in the organization know and understand that strategy? Could they coherently explain it to a complete stranger?

8. Do you agree that North America is undergoing unprecedented change? If yes, what changes have you observed in the last five years? Have these changes affected your ministry? How? How well does your organization handle change?

9. Would you rate your ministry as effective? Why or why not? Would those who are a part of the ministry rate it as effective? Do the people in your ministry understand its bottom line?

10. Does your ministry regularly evaluate itself in any way? If yes, who does the evaluation? Do you believe that it has helped or hindered the ministry? Why?

ENDNOTES

1. Peter F. Drucker, *Management: Tasks, Responsibilities, Practices* (New York: Harper & Row Publishers, 1973), 75.

2. Ibid., 78.

2

The Definition of a Mission
Part 1: What Are We Talking About Anyway?

Pastor Larry Brown left the leadership conference convinced that his church needed a dynamic, biblical mission. He was excited and couldn't wait to tell his board what he had learned. As soon as he arrived home on Friday, he picked up the phone and called all of his board members, asking them to meet with him Sunday after church. He felt that he must persuade them of the importance of a mission while he still sensed it deep within his bones. He desperately needed their support if they were to turn things around in the church. And turn things around they must, or he knew that in time he would move on to more fertile ground.

His concern was that the board might not understand the need for a clear direction nor respond as intensively as he had. The brochure that advertised the conference recommended that pastors bring their board members with them. Too many pastors had attended past conferences alone and returned home only to have the board yawn, stretch, and wonder why they were so excited. The problem was that Pastor Larry decided to attend the conference at the last minute, and his board members had already made other plans. So the responsibility was his.

Let's assume that the board agrees with Pastor Larry and decides that they do need to develop a mission for the church. Precisely what is it that they need to develop? What is the definition of an organizational mission? Chapter 1 was designed to persuade you of the need to develop a mission for your ministry, and hopefully you, like Pastor Larry, are convinced. However, I didn't define what it is that I was talking about. First, this chapter will discuss what a mission isn't. This is important because so much confusion reigns over what should be included in the definition. Then it will define precisely what the mission is. Finally, it will present three different kinds of missions.

WHAT A MISSION IS NOT

Trying to define an organization's mission, whether it's a church ministry, parachurch ministry, or a business, can be problematic. The major reason as cited in the introduction to this book is that other vital concepts like a ministry's values, vision, strategy, definition, and purpose are often confused with mission.

A Mission Is Not a Core Value

Many people confuse an organization's mission with its core values. In an article in *The Washington Post*, the writer confuses the pharmaceutical company Johnson & Johnson's mission with its organizational core values.[1] An organization's core values or credo answers the *why* question: Why do we do what we do? They are important because they drive a ministry or business. They dictate every decision that is made, every conflict that is resolved, and every dollar that is spent.

The mission answers the *what* question: What are we supposed to be doing? The core values supply the reasons for what we do. The mission follows the values in priority and development. It serves to channel our core values into the ministry; it's an expression of our deepest, driving values.

The mission for all churches is the Great Commission (Mark 16:15). The core values are different and will vary from church to church. For example, the core values for the Jerusalem Church are found in Acts 2:42–47 and consist of expository preaching, evangelism, prayer, fellowship, community, praise and worship, and others.

Every ministry will have core values. They may be good or bad values. However, not every ministry has a core mission. In fact, the problem with a number of churches all across North America is that they do not have and may never have had a mission.

A Mission Is Not a Vision

Another concept that many confuse with mission is vision. As I listen to conversations about vision, examine vision statements, and read articles on the concept, I believe that mission and vision are confused more than any other basic ministry concepts. This was the case in the *Leadership* article entitled "A Variety of Visions" that I referred to in the introduction to this book. Confusion arises because much of what people say about the importance of a vision is also true of the mission. Both are vital concepts that are key to any ministry and both deserve our attention. Consequently, a number of statements that leaders assume to be vision statements are actually mission statements, and mixing the two only confuses the distinct vital functions each perform for the organization.

▼▼▼

Much of what people say about the importance of a vision is also true of the mission.

▲▲▲

Untangling the two concepts raises two questions. First, what do a mission and a vision statement have in common? And second, how are the two different? These two questions are critical to understanding the concepts of vision and mission and their importance to a ministry organization. Therefore, I've set aside the next chapter of this book to answer both questions.

For now, my primary purpose is to show how a mission is different from a vision. A mission logically precedes a vision in its development. First, a mission is developed and then it is communicated with a vision. The vision is what the mission looks like when you parade it through your ministry's target community. However, actual experience is that either one may come first. Saying that one should logically come before the other doesn't make it true. Human nature and the creative processes don't always work the way we say they should, and various leaders will affirm that for them the vision came first.

A Mission Is Not a Strategy

A third concept that some confuse with a mission is a strategy. Again, the mission determines what the ministry is supposed to be doing. It is at the very heart of any ministry; it's what God has called the organization to accomplish. The strategy, however, is the actual process that determines how the ministry will accomplish its mission. The mission answers the question, What? while the strategy answers the question, How?

▼▼▼

The strategy is the process that determines how the ministry will accomplish its mission.

▲▲▲

The mission is determinative in formulating the strategy. Thus, logically, it must come before the strategy. Without a mission, the strategy is mostly aimless and often wasted activity. Every ministry has a strategy whether or not it's aware of it. It may be a good strategy or a poor strategy. Regardless, some sort of strategy is in place to implement the activities of the organization no matter how strong or lethargic the organization is.

At this point, perhaps it would be helpful to pause and review what we have learned about the essential ministry elements and their relationships to one another. I began with the ministry's core organizational values. The values come first because they inform and affect all the other vital ministry elements (figure 2.1). They are followed by a church or parachurch's mission, which reflects those values. The mission, in turn, directs both the vision and the strategy. While in some cases the vision could come before the mission, this would never be true of the strategy. You cannot implement what you don't have. It's possible that the strategy could implement the vision, but that is an awkward process at best. It works much better when the strategy implements the mission because both are planning tools, whereas the vision is more for communication purposes. A mission with a bad strategy is impotent. A good strategy with a poor or absent mission is mindless activity.

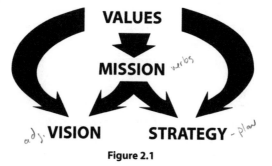

VALUES

MISSION verbs

adj. **VISION**   **STRATEGY** - plan

Figure 2.1

A Mission Is Not a Definition

Some have also confused the mission of a ministry with its definition. They may equate the mission of a church with the definition of a church. A definition defines what an organization such as the church *is*. It concerns its essence or being. For example, some have been very careful to point out that the church is not a building but people. Its very essence is a gathering or community of professing believers in Christ.

The mission defines what the organization has been established to accomplish. It concerns not what it *is*—its essence—but what it *does*—its function. Some definitions may include a statement of function as well as essence. For example, the church could be defined as a gathering of professing believers in Christ (essence) who exist to accomplish Christ's Great Commission (mission). However, a mission should not include a statement of definition as well as function. This only serves to confuse the mission.

A Mission Is Not a Purpose

There aren't many books on organizational mission, and the few that exist or comment on the topic hold that an organization's mission and its purpose are the same. Most don't even attempt to argue the case, they simply assume it. For example, Peter Drucker writes, "Non-profit institutions exist for the sake of their mission. They exist to make a difference in society and the life of the individual. They exist for the sake of their mission, and this must never be forgotten."[2]

However, I see a number of differences between a ministry's mission and its purpose. First, the purpose for a Christian organization such as a church articulates why it exists, why the church is here. The mission of an organization identifies what it's supposed to be doing, not its reason for being. Purpose answers the *why* question; mission, the *what* question: What are we doing? What is our target as a ministry? What are we aiming at?

Second, the term *purpose* implies something more compelling, more fundamental to the ministry than its mission. The purpose isn't simply a target that the organization aims for or the direction in which the ministry is going—it's the organization's entire reason for being. The church or parachurch ministry isn't an end in itself; it serves a much greater purpose—to glorify God. The answer to, What are we supposed to be doing? is the Great Commission (Matt. 28:19–20). That's the church's mission. The answer to, Why are we here? is much broader—it's to glorify God (Pss. 22:23; 50:15; Isa. 24:15; Rom. 15:6; 1 Cor. 6:20; 10:31). That's the church's purpose.

▼▼▼

When a church accomplishes its mission, to make disciples, it serves a broader purpose—it glorifies God.

▲▲▲

Third, the core mission of a church or a parachurch ministry and its core values, vision, and strategy are all subsumed under its purpose. Our purpose on this earth is doxological. We're here to glorify and honor God in all that we do and say. When Christians are Christlike, they enhance the reputation of God and honor him because they are his representatives. When they aren't Christlike, they do damage to God's reputation. They dishonor him. Living Christlike lives is what it means to glorify God. When a church accomplishes its mission, to make disciples, it serves a broader purpose—it glorifies God. The same is true as it lives its core values, realizes its vision, and accomplishes its strategy.

WHAT A MISSION IS

Knowing what the mission isn't helps in discovering what it is because it eliminates other potentially confusing elements. Now it's time to discover what it is. A mission is a broad, brief biblical statement of what the ministry is supposed to be doing. This definition has several key ingredients.

A Mission Is Broad

The first key ingredient is expansiveness. A good mission is broad, overarching, and comprehensive. It's the all-embracing goal, mandate, or charge that takes precedence over all other goals or mandates within the organization. It's the umbrella over all the ministry's activities. It's the predominate thrust that directs all that the organization does. Whatever the ministry attempts must fit under its mission. The biblical mission statements found later in this chapter are broad and all-inclusive. If a parachurch ministry's mission is to evangelize college students, then everything it does should involve evangelism of its target group. If it gets into such areas as discipleship or feeding the hungry, it has strayed beyond its stated mission.

This expansive quality is important because it allows for the flexibility and growth of the institution. In America, the smaller churches are dying and the larger churches are growing even bigger. We're experiencing a megachurch phenomenon. More large churches exist at the dawn of the third millennium than ever before in our nation's history. Lyle Schaller indicates that some four thousand Protestant megachurches have emerged over the past ten to fifteen years.[3] Consequently, when a church is planted today, no one can accurately predict its future. It may quickly plateau and die because of the high risk involved in entrepreneurial ventures, or it may eventually grow into a regional or megachurch. While there are certain principles and practices that aid the ultimate growth and success of a new church start, still no one knows for sure at the front end of the project.[4]

▼▼▼

A good mission must be broad and flexible enough to allow for potential growth.

▲▲▲

My point is that a good mission must be broad and flexible enough to allow for potential growth. With all the helpful information that the church growth movement has supplied over the past two decades, new congregations should plan and expect to grow. Also, plateaued ministries have the potential to redefine their mission and begin to grow as well. Broad missions promote and make room for future growth and versatility. Narrow missions are restrictive and confining. Like a small shoe on a growing child's foot, they inhibit a ministry's normal growth processes.

At the same time, the mission must be focused enough to be clear and set some boundaries for the ministry. It's possible to be so broad that you confuse people and ultimately say nothing. Mission statements that indicate that the church or parachurch ministry exists to glorify God are too broad. They are sound, both biblically and theologically, yet what does it mean to glorify God? Answering this question gets at the purpose of a church and not its mission. I would encourage ministries that insist on using this phrase in their mission statements to explain what it means to glorify God.[5]

A Mission Is Brief

The second key ingredient is brevity. The adjective *brief* is a reference to the size or length of the mission statement. I have heard of mission statements that are fifteen to twenty pages long. Some suggest that it should contain no more than one hundred words. A perusal of the mission statements that appear in Scripture reveals that all are very short. While there is no standard, fixed regulation for the length of such a statement, I would question whether a document that is twenty pages long, or even no more than one hundred words long, really is a mission statement.

How short is brief? A significant, dynamic mission statement need be no longer than a single sentence. As we shall see in the next section, biblical mission statements are approximately a sentence in length. No matter how complex the organization, its leadership should be able to summarize what it's supposed to accomplish in a single, succinct statement. That's not to say that achieving brevity is easy. It requires a careful, thorough understanding of the ministry.

▼▼▼

No matter how complex the organization, its leadership should be able to summarize what it's supposed to accomplish in a single, succinct statement.

▲▲▲

The reason for such brevity is that people will be able to remember a single, well-written sentence. It isn't likely, however, that they will make the effort to remember two or more sentences, much less several pages. The church administrator at Pantego Bible Church in Arlington, Texas, attended a meeting where Peter Drucker was the key speaker. He overheard another participant ask Drucker how long a mission statement should be. Drucker responded, "If you can get the mission statement on a T-shirt, then it's probably the appropriate length."[6] Thus, the critical test for any mission statement is whether it passes the "T-shirt test." Not only is this test an aid to brevity, but should you literally put it on a T-shirt, it would be an aid to communicating the mission statement as well.

A Mission Is Biblical

The third key ingredient is that a mission is based on the Scriptures. God determines what a ministry's mission is. He's the source of your mission, and he reveals this in his Word. Therefore, the precise mission for any ministry is biblically based. The only question is: What does God say that we're supposed to do? A number of missions are sprinkled throughout the Old and New Testament. These broad, brief statements prove to be instructive.

▼▼▼

God determines what a ministry's mission is.

▲▲▲

Mission statements in the Old Testament. A quick survey of the Old Testament surfaces four statements of mission. The first belongs to Adam and Eve. We find their mission statement in Genesis 1:28 which states: "God blessed them and said to them, 'Be fruitful and increase in number; fill the earth and subdue it. Rule over the fish of the sea and the birds of the air and over every living creature that moves on the ground.'" The text is very clear. There is no question that this overarching goal is from God. The first couple is to have dominion over God's newly formed creation.

The second is Moses' mission statement. God reveals his plans to Moses in Exodus 3:7–9, he then commissions him. Verse 10 records God's words to him: "So now, go. I am sending you to Pharaoh to bring my people the Israelites out of Egypt." It's noteworthy that God's plan was to lead his people out of Egyptian slavery and into the Promised Land. However, he commissions Moses to accomplish only their deliverance. God in his wisdom knew that Moses would disobey him and never set foot in the Promised Land. That aspect of God's plan becomes Joshua's mission (Deut. 3:28; 31:7–8; Josh. 1:2).

It's interesting that on several occasions God raises up others to complete someone's mission. God used Joshua, not Moses, to complete his mission for Israel, that is, leading them into the Promised Land. Later in Israel's history, God raised up Elijah, whose mission was to prevail over the prophets and worshippers of Baal (1 Kings 17–18). However, he used Elisha to complete what Elijah had started (2 Kings 2).

The third is David's mission statement. We find it embedded in the Davidic Covenant. The writer of 2 Samuel refers to it in chapter 7, verse 8 where he says: "Now then, tell my servant David, 'This is what the LORD Almighty says: I took you from the pasture and from following the flock to be ruler over my people Israel.'" The writer sheds additional light in 2 Samuel 5:2 where he says: "And the LORD said to you, 'You will shepherd my people Israel, and you will become their ruler.'" God commissioned David to rule and shepherd his people. This involved extending God's sovereign rule over them, their neighbors, and their enemies.

The fourth is Nehemiah's mandate. In Nehemiah 2:17, he says to the people: "Come, let us rebuild the wall of Jerusalem, and we will no longer be in disgrace." Here Nehemiah is telling the distraught remnant what God's mission is for them. The rebuilding of the wall was a physical act replete with spiritual meaning for the struggling nation.

Mission statements in the New Testament. The New Testament as well as the Old provides us with several exemplary mission statements. We'll look at two of the most important ones. The first is the Savior's. Mark 10:45 states: "For even the Son of Man did not come to be served, but to serve, and to give his life as a ransom for many." The same is recorded in Matthew 20:28. Jesus' broad, brief mission was to function as a servant to people, and this service would culminate in the ultimate sacrifice—his death. He was to be the ransom price for humankind as his death would pay the price for their sin.

The second is the mission of the church. It's critical to us because we make up the church; therefore, it's our mission statement. It's what we as Christ's church and body are supposed to be doing. Matthew 28:19 records Jesus' words to his eleven disciples: "Therefore go and make disciples of all nations." Mark 16:15 records the same where the Savior says to his disciples and to us: "Go into all the world and preach the good news to all creation."

▼▼▼

Christ's Great Commission and thus our mission as his church is to make disciples.

▲▲▲

Christ's Great Commission and thus our mission as his church is to make disciples. This involves helping people move from prebirth to maturity. It's a brief, overarching, umbrella statement that includes pursuing lost people (Luke 19:1–10), evangelizing lost people (Mark 16:15), and helping them to move toward maturity or Christlikeness (Matt. 28:19–20). Each person is responsible to accept Christ and then become like him. And Christ has commissioned the church as his organization to help them in this process.[7]

A Mission Is a Statement

The fourth ingredient is that the mission is a statement. A ministry must articulate its comprehensive goal or mandate; otherwise, no one will know what it is much less understand it. This begins with a statement. While this includes a verbal statement, it is most powerful when written down on paper as a visual statement. It's instructive that we know the mission statements of Adam, Moses, and others above because they're visual. The biblical authors have written and recorded them in the pages of Scripture. This is important to mission developers; writing forces you to think and gather your thoughts together. When you record them on paper you should be very clear. If you can't write out your mission, then it's likely not a well-thought-through statement.

▼▼▼

Writing out your mission in the form of a statement puts it into concrete form.

▲▲▲

Writing out your mission in the form of a statement puts it into concrete form. The primary purpose of a written vision statement is to communicate an image of where the church or parachurch ministry is going. The primary purpose of a written mission statement is to communicate concretely where the church or parachurch ministry is going. The difference is that when people read the vision statement, they get an image in their of minds of where the ministry is going, and this serves to motivate or inspire them to move in that direction. It's not as likely that the mission statement will accomplish this. Instead, people will have a clear, succinct statement of the organization's direction that's more for information than inspiration.

A Mission Is What the Ministry Is Supposed to Be Doing

The fifth ingredient is that the mission statement must express what the ministry is to accomplish. It is the ministry's primary task or aim—an expression of intent that informs and gives meaning to the organization. It's what God intends for the ministry to achieve—its basic, essential "business."

The key question is, What is our ministry supposed to be doing? Every ministry must begin with this question. Drucker writes: "We are mission-focused. What are we trying to do? Don't ever forget that first question. The mission must come first. This is the lesson of the last 50–100 years. The moment we lose sight of the mission we are gone."[8] This question is foundational for every church or parachurch organization. It is the *b* of the ministry's ABCs (the *a* is core values and the *c* is vision). We learned that the answer for the church is that it's supposed to be making disciples (Matt. 28:19–20; Mark 16:15). Its mission is to help people move from prebirth to maturity—to come to faith in Christ and mature in him.

▼▼▼

Drucker proves most insightful when he says:
"The moment we lose sight of the mission
we are gone."

▲▲▲

My impression is that not enough of the older, traditional churches born before the 1960s are asking the mission question. Drucker proves most insightful when he says: "The moment we lose sight of the mission we are gone." Commenting on these older American churches, Schaller writes: ". . . two-thirds to three-fourths of all congregations founded before 1960 are either on a plateau or shrinking in numbers."[9]

The question: What is our ministry supposed to be doing? is both aspirational and diagnostic. It serves as an attempt to encourage church and parachurch organizations to consider what they might be missing. It's an excellent question that a potential leader should ask when considering a new ministry such as a pastor candidating at a church. However, this is only the first question. There are several similar diagnostic questions that leaders must ask along with the aspirational one.

What are we doing? It may be that we're a church that is supposed to make disciples. If we're not making disciples, then what are we doing? I've observed that some churches are teaching and becoming cognitive communities that function as mini-seminaries. Some are centers of evangelism the only focus of which is to win the lost. Others are retirement centers for older Christians who feel that they've done their part and now it's time for someone else to take care of them for a change.

How well are we doing what we're doing? Not only are some churches pursuing purposes other than making disciples, but they aren't doing a very good job at what they're doing. This is an issue of quality. They're doing other things and doing them poorly. Scripture teaches what I refer to as a theology of excellence—that whatever we do, we must do it as to the Lord, whether it's our worship (Lev. 22:20–22; Num. 18:29–30) or our work (Eph. 6:7; Col. 3:23). Ultimately, we'll be judged according to the quality of our works (1 Cor. 3:13). This is also an issue of outreach. People are looking for ministries that do what they do well. They will be turned off by a ministry that does its work sloppily.

Why aren't we doing what we're supposed to be doing? If we're a church, this question is an attempt to get at the heart of why we aren't obeying Christ's clear command to make disciples. Numerous answers exist. As a church grows in size and adds a mortgage payment and staff salaries, it may focus inward and promptly forget the Great Commission. The pastor may be strong in some area such as preaching, emphasizing it over the other responsibilities of the Great Commission. Some additional answers are disobedience, ignorance, hidden agendas, power plays, laziness, and so on.

What will it take for this ministry to do what it's supposed to be doing? Next to the first question, this is the most important mission question an evangelical organization can ask. It's also vital to a person who is considering the leadership of a plateaued or declining ministry. The answer dictates whether the church will obey Christ. The answer will also dictate the future of the church. I'm inclined to believe that if a church knows what its biblical mission is but persists in pursuing other interests, then over time God will not bless but discipline it. And long term disobedience may result in death (Rev. 2–3).

THE KINDS OF MISSIONS

In an attempt to come up with a pragmatic, functional definition that will help guide our ministries we have discovered what a mission is as well as what it isn't. We can further enhance our understanding of this concept by looking at the different kinds of missions. We'll examine three: personal, organizational, and departmental.

The Personal Mission

The personal mission is as important to the individual as the organizational mission is to a ministry. Your personal mission answers a similar question to an organizational mission: What am I supposed to be doing? or better: What does God want me to do with my life? It has much to do with what is most important in your life, or what you care about in your life as a whole. The value of a personal mission is that it can make the difference between being average for Christ and being exceptional for him. In the context of the business world, one person expresses it this way: "I believe it's true that the difference between great people and everyone else is that great people create their lives actively, while everyone else is created *by* their lives, passively waiting to see where life takes them next."[10] Developing your personal mission allows you to create your life actively.

▼▼▼

The value of a personal mission is that it can make the difference between being average for Christ and being exceptional for him.

▲▲▲

I would encourage you to write a personal ministry mission statement. My personal mission is to prepare a new generation of leaders for significant, high impact ministry in the twenty-first century. The following are some important questions that will help you: What do you want to do with your life? If God gave you one wish for your life, what would you choose? What does God want you to do with your life? In light of your gifts and talents, how could you best serve the Savior? What legacy do you want to leave behind? If someone honored you with a testimonial dinner, what would people say about you? Long after you're gone, what will people such as your family and friends remember most about you?[11]

The Organizational Mission

This book is all about organizational missions. You might also describe them as corporate, congregational, or institutional missions. They ask: What is the mission of a church or parachurch ministry? I intentionally discuss the missions of other organizations such as those found in the marketplace because they are instructive and tend to be anywhere from ten to twenty years ahead of the typical traditional church. They often prove most helpful but must be run through a biblical, theological grid.

In some situations such as the church, the organizational mission is supposed to help implement the individual mission statements of those who are a part of it. As cited above, the church's mission is to make disciples or assist its people as they do everything in the Spirit's power to become Christ's disciples. In some parachurch works, the organization's mission may be more focused than its members' personal missions. This would apply to a parachurch ministry that majors in evangelism. Certainly God wants his people to do evangelism, and their personal mission includes but goes beyond their ministry's mission.

The Departmental Mission

Once your ministry has prepared its organizational mission, it should ask each department within to develop its own mission statement. The organizational mission serves as the broad umbrella for the entire ministry. The departmental missions must fit somewhere under that umbrella. It presents what each department is supposed to be doing that contributes to the effectiveness of the entire organization. This serves to bring the mission concept down to the grassroots level.

The following is a sample departmental mission statement developed by the physical plant at Dallas Theological Seminary in Dallas, Texas:

> The Physical Plant's mission is to serve the Dallas Theological Seminary community with a professional and personable attitude by providing a physical environment which is conducive to the DTS mission of preparing godly servant-leaders in the body of Christ worldwide.

QUESTIONS FOR THOUGHT AND DISCUSSION

1. Are you serving in a church or parachurch ministry? Does it have a mission statement? Why or why not?

2. What is your ministry actually doing? Does this line up with what it's supposed to be doing? Explain.

3. How well is your ministry doing what it's doing? Do the leaders believe that it's important to pursue excellence in whatever you're doing? Why or why not? Do your people believe that it's important to pursue excellence in ministry? Why or why not?

4. What will it take for your ministry to change and do what Christ wants it to do? Is the leadership willing to move in a new direction? Are the people willing to move in a new direction? Are you willing to do whatever it takes to move in a new direction?

5. Have you developed a personal mission statement? If not, are you convinced that you should do this? Why or why not? How might it help you at this point in your life and ministry?

ENDNOTES

1. Jay Matthews, "Much Ado About Nothing?" *The Washington Post*, 8 January 1995.

2. Peter F. Drucker, *Managing the Non-Profit Organization* (New York: Harper Business, 1990), 45.

3. Lyle E. Schaller, *The New Reformation* (Nashville: Abingdon Press, 1995), 13.

4. These are found in my book *Planting Growing Churches for the 21st Century* (Grand Rapids: Baker Book House, 1992).

5. I spend some time clarifying what this phrase means from a biblical perspective in chapter three of my book *Vision America* (Grand Rapids: Baker Book House, 1995).

6. Randy Frazee with Lyle E. Schaller, *The Comeback Congregation* (Nashville: Abingdon Press, 1995), 6.

7. I discuss the biblical concept of making disciples in *Strategy 2000* (Grand Rapids: Kregel Publications, 1996).

8. "The New Models," *NEXT* 1, no. 2 (August 1995): 2.

9. Frazee with Schaller, *The Comeback Congregation*, 11.

10. Michael Gerber, *The E-Myth* (New York: Harper Business, 1986), 85.
11. I have written *Maximizing Your Effectiveness* (Grand Rapids: Baker Book House, 1995) to help people think through these issues and more.

3

The Definition of a Mission
Part 2: Is It a Vision or a Mission?

As a leader and pastor, Larry Brown has the awesome responsibility of leading Grace Community Church to discover and craft its mission. His ability to accomplish this task will probably mean the difference between the success or failure of this ministry over the next five to ten years. Perhaps in his tenure at Grace, he'll accomplish little more than helping the church articulate and own a compelling mission. However, if he does this and little more, his ministry will be a success.

While he was convinced, Pastor Larry wondered if he would be able to convince his board of the church's need for a mission. They must gain ownership, or it would not happen. He met with the board only to discover that they, like he, sensed that something vital was missing. When he pointed to the church's need for a mission, most responded warmly and enthusiastically. What he discovered was that most on the board shared some familiarity with modern day management concepts. Only they, like many other church board members, weren't sure if it was appropriate to apply some of these marketplace principles to the church. Pastor Larry took great pains to explain his understanding of the mission concept. As in chapter 2, he explained first what it isn't and then what it is.

The one sticking point in the entire meeting, however, was the difference between a mission and a vision. Two of the members worked for Fortune 500 firms that required its upper management to attend various leadership seminars. Both had recently attended the same seminar on vision, and they didn't understand how the two were different. Others on the board were somewhat familiar with the topic and voiced similar confusion.

The board of Grace Community Church is not alone in this quandary. We have already seen in the earlier chapters that some confusion does exist. The problem is that both an organizational mission and vision have some commonalities and some distinctives. This chapter will seek to sharpen the definition of a mission by examining the similarities and differences of an organizational mission and vision. How are they alike and how are they different?

THE SIMILARITIES OF A MISSION AND VISION

A mission and a vision are similar in four ways: Both are biblically based, direction oriented, goal directed, and future focused.

A Mission and a Vision Are Biblically Based

Both the leader's and the ministry's mission must come from God. For those whose hearts beat for Christ, no other source will do. While it's possible that God might reveal a mission in some unnatural, subjective way, most will find it in the Bible. The same is true of the vision. Consequently, both a mission and vision are biblically based.

I presented several biblical mission statements from both the Old and New Testament in chapter 2. One from the Old Testament was the mission that God gave to Moses for his people Israel. Moses' commission is recorded in Exodus 3:10 where God commands him: "So now, go. I am sending you to Pharaoh to bring my people the Israelites out of Egypt."

In the same chapter, God is also the source of Moses' vision for Israel. He records it in Exodus 3:7–8: "The LORD said, 'I have indeed seen the misery of my people in Egypt. I have heard them crying out because of their slave drivers, and I am concerned about their suffering. So I have come down to rescue them from the hand of the Egyptians and to bring them up out of that land into a good and spacious land, a land flowing with milk and honey—the home of the Canaanites, Hittites, Amorites, Perizzites, Hivites and Jebusites.'"

God repeats this vision periodically as Israel travels toward the Promised Land (Deut. 8:7–10; 11:9–12). This repetition serves to regularly remind the Israelites of the vision, to inspire them along the way as they face various obstacles, and to remind them that God is the source of their mission and vision.

A Mission and a Vision Are Direction Oriented

A second factor that a mission and vision have in common is that they are both directional; they provide a direction for the ministry. As I survey the North American church scene, I have observed that most churches fall into three categories in terms of directional problems. The largest category is churches that are directionless. If you were to ask the board or the pastor the *direction* question, Where are you going? they wouldn't be able to give you a clear answer. Most of these are maintenance ministries that, like crippled ships at sea, are headed nowhere.

A second category is churches with multiple directions. Usually the pastor is pulling in one direction while the various people on the board are each pulling in a different direction. It's only a matter of time before they pull apart. They are like the tides and wind that push and pull a crippled ship at sea, constantly changing its course and moving it in different directions.

The last category is churches that are moving in the same direction only it's the wrong direction. These are churches that specialize in some area that fits under the umbrella of the Great Commission rather than the Commission itself, such as the teaching church or the soul-winning church. They are like a ship at sea that isn't crippled but moving full speed ahead. The only problem is that they're steaming toward the wrong port.

It's imperative that leaders know where they are taking their ministries. This means that they must know their own direction. I would define a Christian leader as (1) a godly servant who (2) knows where God wants him or her to go and (3) has followers. The first part of the definition reflects on the leader's character, the third on the leader's ability to influence people. The second has everything to do with his or her direction. You must have a clear sense of direction; you must know where you're going if you plan to lead people.

▼▼▼

It's imperative that leaders know where they are taking their ministries.

▲▲▲

As stated in chapter 1, the mission of a ministry organization answers the question: Where are we going? However, the vision also answers the directional question. Many would argue that churches and parachurch ministries are vision-driven. I believe that they are vision-focused and values-driven. The vision serves not to drive the organization but to bring its direction into focus. I demonstrate this function in the classroom by putting a transparency on an overhead projector that is out of focus to the point that no one can read it. Then I gradually adjust the projector until the transparency comes into focus. This is what the vision does for a ministry—it's all about focusing its direction. It's the values, however, not the vision, that drive the ministry in a particular direction. The core organizational values dictate every decision the organization makes, every dollar it spends, and many other vital areas.[1] Values are the engine that powers the ship to move toward its port.

The Mission and Vision Are Goal Directed

In chapter 1, we found that the mission helps a church or parachurch ministry determine its biblical function. It answers the question: What are we supposed to be doing? In chapter 2, we discovered that for the church, the answer to this question is the Great Commission. Consequently, in planning terminology, the overarching, all-encompassing goal of the church is the Great Commission.

The same is true for a ministry's vision. The mission and the vision are not only directional, they are functional. Let's continue to use the church as an example. The vision of the church, like the mission, is the Great Commission, for God has predetermined both. He has provided the mission in Matthew 28:19–20; Mark 16:15; Luke 24:47–48; and Acts 1:8. What the mission looks like when the church realizes it in the future is the vision. As a mission, it's broad and brief; as a vision, it's clear and challenging.

What, then, is the Great Commission? Matthew 28:19–20 says it's to go and make disciples. Mark 16:15 says that it's to go into all the world and preach the Good News to everyone. Therefore, the Great Commission involves pursuing lost people, winning them, and then leading them to maturity or Christlikeness. Great Commission churches aren't evangelistic headhunter institutions. Their directing goal is to make disciples—to see ungodly pagans who are totally focused on themselves become godly committed Christians who are totally focused on the Savior. This umbrella mandate directs and informs all that the church does.

A Mission and a Vision Are Future Focused

In chapter 1, we learned that a ministry's mission has everything to do with the future. While a ministry may learn from the past (its failures as well as its successes), it must not live in the past (Phil. 3:13–14). Whenever a ministry crafts its mission statement, it is inventing and defining its future. For you not to do so can mean two things: you may not have a future, or you may be allowing someone or something else to define your future for you. Both are frightening and unacceptable.

A ministry's vision also has everything to do with the future. A vision is a clear, challenging picture of the future of your ministry. The mission is the end result; the vision is a mental snapshot of the end result. If people want to know what a ministry will look like ten to twenty years from now, then they need to examine its vision statement. If they can close their eyes and picture in their minds the future the vision statement describes, then that's the vision for the ministry. It is a mental picture of the potential, desirable future state of the organization. It's a window to the church's tomorrow.

Leaders often speak of accomplishing the mission and/or the vision. An organization can only accomplish a portion of its mission and vision. This is because both live in the future; they are perpetually in a state of becoming, and thus remain future focused. For example, the Great Commission is both the mission and vision of the church. While a church may reach and disciple even a large number of people, it will never fully accomplish the Commission. The church is attempting to accomplish and does accomplish what it cannot totally accomplish. This is a paradox that exists because of the future orientation of the mission and vision concepts.

A SUMMARY OF THE SIMILARITIES BETWEEN A MISSION AND A VISION
Biblically based
Direction oriented
Goal directed
Future focused

THE DIFFERENCES BETWEEN A MISSION AND A VISION

The differences between a mission and a vision outweigh the similarities. This section covers twelve of these differences.

The Definition of a Mission and a Vision

The first major difference between a mission and a vision is their meanings. I define an organization's mission differently from its vision. In chapter 2, the definition of a mission is that it's a broad, brief biblical statement of what the ministry is supposed to be doing. Whereas a mission is broad, a vision is detailed. The mission paints a broad brush stroke of the future, and the vision fills in the details. The mission is also brief. An aspect of its power is its brevity. It gets to the point. What it does, it does quickly and succinctly. However, a vision's impact is its length—it takes more time to unfold but allows the hearer to savor and participate more fully in the organization's preferred future.

▼▼▼

The mission paints a broad brush stroke of the future,
and the vision fills in the details.

▲▲▲

I define a vision in several different ways. One that relates to the concept of mission and helps to better discern the differences between the mission and the vision is the following: The vision is what the ministry will look like as it accomplishes its mission in its unique ministry community. It's a snapshot or picture carried in your mental billfold or purse of what the ministry is supposed to be doing.

There are several definitional characteristics that distinguish the two. One is that the mission precedes the vision in order. If the vision is "what the mission looks like," then logically the mission must already be in existence. Second, the vision is a "seeing" concept, whereas the mission is a "doing" concept. Third, the mission won't change significantly, whereas the vision will change depending on the uniqueness of the "particular ministry's community." The following section will discuss some of these differing characteristics in more detail.

The Application of a Mission and a Vision

Another key difference between a ministry's mission and its vision is their application. I use the term *application* to mean what they do for the ministry. The application of the mission to the organization is in the area of planning. It's a planning tool. The mission comes first; it precedes the plan. They work together like an engine of a locomotive and its caboose. If you don't have a mission, then you can't have a plan. Some may throw something together and call it a plan, but without a mission that provides direction, a plan is anemic and impotent. A ship may steam all around the ocean, but without a port, it accomplishes little more than a nice view of a lot of salt water and some fantastic sunsets.

The application of the vision to the ministry is primarily in the area of communication. The mission is vital to an organization's planning, while the vision is vital to the articulation of its direction and future. How does a church or parachurch ministry communicate to its members and constituency where it's going in such a way that everyone has a mental snapshot before they arrive? The answer is by casting an ideal, unique vision. As we invent and define the future of our ministries, all need a mental picture of what it will look like as we begin the journey and as we move toward that mental image. This is why God gave Moses the vision for Israel before they began the long, arduous journey, and then continued to recast the vision while they were on that journey. It's true that Israel meandered all over the Sinai. However, that was because of the people's disobedience, not their lack of vision.

▼▼▼

The mission is vital to an organization's planning, while the vision is vital to the articulation of its direction and future.

▲▲▲

A church may communicate its vision in numerous ways.[2] The only limit to vision communication is the creative ability of the communicator. However, the primary form is verbal as when a pastor preaches a sermon. Much as Dr. Martin Luther King's "I Have a Dream" speech created a visual, mental picture in people's minds of what racial equality in America might look like, a pastor's sermon creates a visual, mental picture in people's minds of what the church's future will look like.

The Length of a Mission and a Vision

Every organization should be able to articulate its mission in a written statement. And that statement should be brief. Some companies have mission statements that are as long as ten to fifteen pages. And some advise that you limit your mission statement to one hundred words. In the last chapter, I suggested that *brief* means that it can pass the "T-shirt test." It should be short enough in length that it can fit on a T-shirt.

Any church or parachurch ministry, as well as any company that's competing in the marketplace, should be able to summarize its mission statement in a single sentence. This means that it will have to be a broad statement, but that is okay, for the mission statement is broad by definition. The reason for brevity is twofold. First, a single sentence mission statement is easy to remember. Second, the less that is said, the less confusion there will be over the organizational mission.

While you might communicate the vision more effectively in other ways, you should be able to write it down on a piece of paper in the form of a statement. However, it won't pass the "T-shirt test." And that is another major difference between the vision and the mission. The vision by nature will be longer. In fact, if your vision is only a couple of sentences long, then it's not a vision, it's a mission statement.

When consulting with denominations and churches in the area of vision, I ask them to write out their vision statements. This forces them to think carefully and specifically about the future of their ministries and how they want to communicate it to their people. I ask them to close their eyes and describe on paper what they see or want to see as they envision their ministries five, ten, or fifteen years from now. No one has ever accomplished this assignment with one sentence. It's usually from several sentences to as much as a page or two in length.

The Purpose of a Mission and a Vision

A fourth difference is the mission's purpose. It's not the same as that of the vision. The purpose of a well-thought-through, dynamic mission is to inform. Again, it answers the *functional* question: What are we supposed to be doing? What is the primary task to which God has called us? Where do we want to focus our energies as a ministry? It expresses the task of the ministry organization. The mission of the church is to make disciples (Matt. 28:19–20). The mission of the evangelistic parachurch ministry is to win souls. The articulation of a ministry's mission is the way it informs people of its function or what its primary task is all about.

The purpose of a credible, attractive vision is to inspire. To some degree a vision, like the mission, informs people of the ministry's direction. And to some degree, a well-written mission statement can inspire people. But these aren't nor should they be the primary purposes of either concept. When a church or parachurch casts its vision, that process serves to inspire people to respond—to do what they're supposed to do. It captures the imagination and engages the spirit. A well-articulated, biblical vision has the power to inspire not only a decision to follow but, more important, a commitment to follow the direction of the leadership.

A vision has the power to motivate people to action, to produce the results that the mission calls for. It reaches out and touches the need within all of us for a sense of significance and meaning in life. We sincerely desire that what we do, our servanthood, will make a difference, that it will count for something special and important to the Savior. The vision helps to accomplish that purpose.

The Activity of a Mission and a Vision

A fifth difference between a mission and a vision is activity. Activity is what actually happens when a ministry implements its mission or vision. The activity of the mission is doing or action. It is action that brings accomplishments or results. This is because the mission is tied so closely with planning and strategy, and it's the purpose of the strategy to accomplish the mission. The mission of the church is the Great Commission. It results in activity—moving people from prebirth to maturity. If the desired result isn't happening, then something is wrong with the mission.

The activity of the vision, however, isn't doing but seeing. When a leader casts the vision, people should be able to see the ideal, unique future of the ministry. As passion is a "feeling" concept, so vision is a "seeing" concept. It enables people to carry around a snapshot of the future of the ministry in their mental purses or billfolds. The process of articulating the vision should ultimately lead to doing, but that isn't what it's designed to accomplish. Over a period of vision casting, you want those in your ministry to respond with the words, "I see . . . I see what you're talking about." If your people cannot see it, it probably won't happen!

The vision development process, like the mission development process, involves writing the vision down on a piece of paper. In helping pastors and seminarians develop their visions, I ask them to close their eyes and write what they see when they think about their ministries in the future. I've found that what they write down initially isn't visual enough. Thus, I keep asking them: What does it look like?

The Source of a Mission and a Vision

A sixth way that a mission is distinct from a vision is its source. The source of the mission is the head. Mission is something that's cognitive—you think about it. It concerns the ideas stored in your head; it involves cognition or comprehension. You must think, ask questions, and, if necessary, do some research. You should investigate the Scriptures to determine if they dictate the mission of your organization, whether it's ministry or marketplace oriented. The result of communicating your mission statement is understanding.

▼▼▼

The source of the vision isn't the head but the heart. It touches not so much the intellect but the imagination.

▲▲▲

The source of the vision isn't the head but the heart. It touches not so much the intellect but the imagination. While you may see it in your mind, it comes from your heart. This is the emotional side of the vision. You aren't likely to get emotional over your mission statement, but you should over your vision statement. In eliciting a mental picture of your preferred future, the vision should reach into your heart and touch your emotions. To a certain extent, the vision serves as a time machine to transport you into the future, and the result is that you both see and feel your future.

This underlines the importance of the vision statement for your ministry. When people not only understand where you're going, but see and feel it, then they are more likely to decide not only in favor of it but to commit to it. And commitment is crucial, because a decision is short term, lasting only for a few days at best; a commitment is long term and could last for one's lifetime.

The Order of a Mission and a Vision

A seventh way in which a ministry's mission may be distinct from its vision is their order. The question is: Which came first, the mission or the vision? Essentially, it's the same question as: Which came first, the chicken or the egg? The definition that I used previously states that a vision is what the mission looks like as it's uniquely realized in the ministry's community. According to this definition, the mission logically and sequentially precedes the vision. The leader creates his or her mission first. Next, the vision is what you see as you consider the implementation of the mission. The mission is there first, and the vision serves to picture it, to flesh out its details.

▼▼▼

The mission logically and
sequentially precedes the vision.

▲▲▲

However, the human creative processes don't always function according to our definitions or the way we think they should. Sometimes God gives a leader a vision first and provides a mission later, especially if that leader is a strong visionary. A visionary regularly sees things in his or her mind; visionaries carry ideas and images around in their imaginations. Consequently, it's very possible that the vision might precede the mission.

The Coherence of a Mission and a Vision

The eighth way that a mission is different from a vision is coherence. A church's mission will remain consistent over a long period of time. Essentially it hasn't changed since Christ gave it in Matthew 28:19–20. Its wording may be different and should vary from church to church, but the core is the same—to make disciples. The reason some churches have inconsistent missions is because they have the wrong missions. They are like those ships that are steaming at full speed toward the wrong port.

The church's vision, however, will vary from institution to institution. Since the vision is what you see as the church uniquely realizes its mission in a particular ministry community, each church will have a different vision. This is because no community is alike. Each community represents a unique culture that has certain values, norms, heroes, symbols, traditions, and so on. As a church envisions winning and discipling various people from rich to poor and of all nationalities, the vision couldn't possibly be consistent from one to another.

The Focus of a Mission and a Vision

A ninth distinction between the mission and the vision is focus. The focus of the mission is broad and general. It presents the overall, comprehensive goal of the ministry. It should not present any details or ministry minutiae. You get none of the particulars. If you wanted to make a film of the ministry's mission, the camera would have to back off and shoot from a distance. Because the mission is broad, every other goal and every potential goal should fall under it as the overarching goal of the ministry. If something doesn't fit, then it should be discarded. This expansiveness of the mission makes the ministry flexible to allow for positive, beneficial change and growth.

The focus of the vision is narrow. This helps leaders clearly see their target. If you filmed a ministry's vision, the camera would move up close to capture the details. In his book, *Hey, Wait a Minute,* former football coach John Madden presents Vince Lombardi's answer to the question: What's the difference between a good and a bad coach? Lombardi's reply: "The best coaches know what the end result looks like, whether it's an offensive play, a defensive play, a defensive coverage, or just some area of the organization. If you don't know what the end result is supposed to look like, you can't get there."[3] The vision provides the necessary focus so that good leaders as well as good football coaches know what the end result looks like.

The vision may provide a more detailed picture of the people you intend to reach, such as collegians, older adults, or children; the ministry community such as African Americans, Hispanics, Anglos, or a mixture of the same; the geographical area like wooded, mountainous, ocean front, inner city; people relating to one another, for example, people coming to faith, families being reunited, the restoration of broken relationships; and the facilities such as a school, storefront, YMCA, house, or a church building.

The Effect of the Mission and the Vision

A tenth distinction is the effect of the mission and the vision. The effect of the mission is to clarify what the ministry is supposed to be doing. Formulating a mission forces the leadership and the constituency of a church to carefully examine what the ministry is doing in light of what it's supposed to be doing. The primary tool of the process is questions, like those raised at the end of chapter 2: What are we supposed to be doing? What are we doing? Why aren't we doing what we're supposed to be doing? What will it take to do what we're supposed to be doing?

It also forces the leadership and constituency of the parachurch ministry to clarify its mission. The Savior has already predetermined the church's mission. This isn't the case for the parachurch. Consequently, the latter has several different missions to choose from. If it's evangelistic in nature, then whom will it evangelize? The mission will force it to make what may be some difficult but necessary choices that will clarify what the ministry is all about.

▼▼▼

The mission helps us to determine what we're to be doing, and the vision challenges us to see ourselves doing it.

▲▲▲

The effect of the vision isn't to clarify but to challenge. Rather than clarify what it is our ministry is supposed to do, the vision challenges us to see what we're supposed to do. I also define a vision as a clear, challenging picture of the future of our ministry as we believe it can and must be.[4] The mission helps us to determine what we're to be doing, and the vision challenges us to see ourselves doing it. In this sense, it serves to probe and prod us to action. Leaders and vision casters use the vision to "throw down" the proverbial gauntlet in front of their people, challenging them to activity.

The Development of a Mission and a Vision

The eleventh difference between a mission and a vision is the development of each. The question is, How do you develop a mission and a vision? The development of a dynamic, compelling ministry mission is like a science. Thus, it's more taught than caught. The mission statement is rational, straightforward, objective, and concrete; therefore, it's much easier to teach. Once you've seen a few samples, you have a good feel for how to develop and articulate a mission statement for your ministry, and the process doesn't consume a lot of your time.

The development of the ministry vision, however, is more like an art. That means that it's more caught than taught. The development of a clear, challenging vision is intuitive. It seems to come from nowhere and simply "pops" into one's head. It's a subjective, abstract concept. This means that it's more difficult to develop and articulate. It also takes longer to develop—it's wrapped in the foil of creativity and baked in the oven of time. Consequently, visionary people will have an easier time developing a vision for their ministries, whereas less visionary people have a difficult time catching the process.

The Communication of a Mission and a Vision

A final distinctive is how a ministry communicates its mission and vision. This distinctive assumes that leaders need to communicate both concepts. The question is, What's the most effective way to communicate each?

The primary way to communicate your ministry mission is in a concrete written form. Some good ways to propagate your mission statement is to place it on a T-shirt; print it on an attractive wall plaque that you place in a highly visible location such as the foyer, elevator, doors, or office walls; publish it in the bulletin, a brochure, or the ministry's newsletter. More on this in chapter 6.

The chief way to cast your ministry vision is verbal. The end is visual (a vision), but the means to that end is verbal. You may attempt to write it out as you would the mission statement, but this isn't as easy as verbalizing it. It's most effective when it's spoken or preached. That's why the pulpit is such a good platform from which pastors and leaders may cast a ministry's vision. When a new American president communicates his vision to the nation, he does so initially at his inaugural in the form of a speech. Next, he reports on the progress that he's made in implementing the vision in his yearly State of the Union message. This event also provides an opportunity to regularly recast his vision. He chooses to communicate his vision in spoken words, regardless of all the technology that's available to him.

A CHART OF THE DIFFERENCES
BETWEEN A MISSION AND A VISION

	Mission	Vision
1. Definition	Statement	Snapshot
2. Application	Planning	Communication
3. Length	Short	Long
4. Purpose	Informs	Inspires
5. Activity	Doing	Seeing
6. Source	Head	Heart
7. Order	First	Second
8. Coherence	Common	Unique
9. Focus	Broad	Narrow
10. Effect	Clarifies	Challenges
11. Development	Science (taught)	Art (caught)
12. Communication	Visual	Verbal

QUESTIONS FOR THOUGHT AND DISCUSSION

1. As you think about your ministry's present mission and vision or a potential mission and vision, are they both from God? How do you know? Can you support them from the Scriptures? If yes, what passages? If no, why not?

2. Do your mission and vision provide a direction for your ministry? If yes, what is that direction. If no, why not? Is the pastor or ministry leader moving in the direction of the mission and vision? Why or why not? Is the board doing the same? Why or why not?

3. Do the mission and vision provide a clear, preferred future for your ministry? If yes, what is that future? If no, why not, and does the ministry have a future if it doesn't have a mission and/ or a vision?

4. Does your mission provide a dynamic statement of what your ministry is supposed to be doing? Why or why not? Does your vision provide a snapshot of what your mission looks like as it's realized in your ministry community? Why or why not?

5. Does your ministry use the mission to lead in all its planning? Why or why not? Does the ministry use the vision as a means of communicating its direction and its future? Why or why not?

6. Is your mission statement shorter or longer than your vision statement? Which do you believe should be longer? Why? Is the purpose of your mission to inform your people what you're supposed to be doing? Why or why not? Is the purpose of your vision statement to inspire your people to do what they're supposed to be doing? Why or why not?

7. There are several potential missions for any ministry. Does your mission clarify for your people what your particular mission is? If no, why not? Does your vision challenge your people to implement the mission of the ministry? Why or why not? How do you know?

8. As you've thought about and developed your mission, has the process been difficult? Why or why not? As you've done the same with your vision, has the process been difficult? Why or why not? Which has been easiest to understand and develop, the mission or the vision? Why? Would you agree or disagree with the statement: "The vision is more caught than taught." Explain.

9. As you've attempted to communicate your mission to people, has it been more verbal or visual? What are some of the methods that you've used to communicate your mission? As you've articulated your vision, has it been more verbal or visual? What are some of the methods that you've used to communicate your vision? Would you agree that the communication of the mission lends itself more to a concrete written approach, and the vision to a spoken approach?

ENDNOTES

1. See Aubrey Malphurs, *Values-Driven Leadership* (Grand Rapids: Baker Book House, 1996), chap. 2.

2. I provide a number of examples in chapter 5 of *Developing a Vision for Ministry in the 21st Century* (Grand Rapids: Baker Book House, 1992).

3. John Madden with D. Anderson, *Hey, Wait a Minute: I Wrote a Book* (New York: Ballentine, 1985), 225–26.

4. Aubrey Malphurs, *Developing a Vision for Ministry in the 21st Century* (Grand Rapids: Baker Book House, 1992).

4

The Development of the Mission
Part 1: Four Steps for Writing Your Own
Mission Statement

Pastor Larry Brown was surprised and delighted at his board's response to the need for a dynamic ministry mission. He had anticipated some resistance, especially from two of the older leaders. As he thought about it later, he realized that his perception of them had been unfair. He had assumed that because they were older, they would be resistant to new ideas. While sometimes that is the case, it's not always the case. He had misjudged these individuals. Later, he found them to be two of his staunchest supporters in the church.

After some discussion, the board agreed that the mission concept wasn't only a marketplace idea, but that it was biblical and appropriate for the church. Pastor Larry had taken some notes at the leadership seminar that established the biblical basis for developing a ministry mission. He provided copies of the material for the board that helped the members think through the issue theologically. You can peek over their shoulders if you review the information in chapter 2. While they didn't completely understand the difference between a mission and a vision, they grasped enough to see the importance of developing both for their ministry and agreed to pursue the same quickly.

How did they go about developing a mission statement? Mission development consists of the four *ps*: preparation, personnel, process, and product. This chapter will help you think through the first three. You will discover the importance of preparing for the process, who should be involved in the process, and finally what the process itself consists of. Chapter 5 deals with the fourth *p*—the product.

THE PREPARATION FOR DEVELOPING A MISSION

The process of formulating the mission statement for a ministry is critical. Thus, it would be a major mistake to jump immediately into the mission development process without first preparing those leaders who will be a part of that process. At Grace Community Church, the leaders are Pastor Larry and the board. Their preparation consists of five elements.

1. The Need for a Mission

One of the first questions the board must ask as it prepares to develop its mission is, Do we sincerely believe that we need a core organizational mission? If they aren't convinced of the need, then they're wasting everyone's time. Even if they develop an excellent mission, they will virtually ignore it, and no one will benefit from it. The mission will experience an early ministry retirement, and a secretary will eventually bury it somewhere under "m" in the church's filing cabinet.

This isn't the problem at Grace Community Church. The entire board sees the need for a ministry mission. However, they are not representative of many churches sprinkled all across North America. How do you help people see their need for a mission? How do you convince them of such a need? A good way is to conduct a mission audit. The following vital questions will help ministry leaders understand their need for a dynamic mission (see appendix A for a working copy).

The Mission Audit

- According to the Scriptures or the founding mission, what is this ministry supposed to be doing?
- What is it really doing?
- If your answers to 1 and 2 are different, then how do you explain the discrepancy?
- If the ministry ship continues on its present course, where will it dock in the next few years? Is this good or bad?
- Do your key leaders know where the ministry is going? Do all agree on that direction?
- Assuming the ministry is off course, what would it take for it to change course and begin doing what it's supposed to be doing?
- Do you believe this will happen? Why or why not? If so, when?
- Are you and all key leaders willing to do whatever it takes to move in a different direction? If not, why?

The most important time to design and develop a dynamic mission statement is either at the very beginning of your ministry or while it is successful. However, success can be a major hindrance to seeing the need for a core organizational mission. When a ministry is successful, people are least convinced of the need for any kind of change, whether it's the development of a mission statement or something else. So asking the mission question is difficult. Everyone in the church or parachurch thinks that the answer is so obvious as not to merit discussion. It's not popular to argue with success. As the old saying goes, "If it ain't broke, don't fix it!" But success is a poor teacher at best. It seduces leaders into thinking they can't fail strategically or morally. And it's an unrealistic guide to the future, for present success is no guarantee of future success.

However, to wait until the ministry is in trouble to articulate a mission is to play Russian roulette with God's work. To wait until the ministry ship is badly listing or sinking may be too late. But another old saying, "better late than never" applies here. While a mission is no genie in a bottle, the development of a ministry direction has bailed out some failing church and parachurch ministries.

▼▼▼

*To wait until the ministry is in trouble
to articulate a mission is to play
Russian roulette with God's work.*

▲▲▲

2. The Readiness for a Mission

Once a ministry sees its need for a mission, then most often it's ready to develop the same. However, this isn't always the case. At least three major barriers exist to developing a succinct mission.

Leaders think their ministry situation is an exception. Leaders in this category believe and even argue that their ministry is too old, too small, too rural, or too anything (you fill in the blank) to develop a dynamic mission, even if they see the need for one. A parallel example is people who smoke. If you ask them why they take up smoking or continue to smoke after all the warnings and negative statistics from the Surgeon General, you'll discover that most think they're invincible—they'll be the exception.

▼▼▼

Once a ministry sees its need for a mission,
then most often it's ready to develop the same.

▲▲▲

I believe that those who somehow see their ministries as the exceptions to the norm need a mission the most. Often their reluctance is a veiled attempt to mask their fear of the new, the future, and the unknown, or to cover their feelings of incompetence and failure whether perceived or actual.

Procrastination. Some leaders put off the development of a core ministry mission because of their workload. They already have more work or ministry to accomplish than is possible. Thus, the idea of another project such as a mission statement, though important, becomes the proverbial straw that breaks the camel's back.

Other leaders procrastinate because of the fear of failure. To cultivate an organizational mission is to establish its overarching goal. In most good planning, evaluation takes place, and the basis for evaluating the organization is the accomplishment of the mission or goal. Consequently, the leader may ask, What if we don't accomplish the mission? Instead of looking like a failure, the leader simply delays the process until everyone forgets about it.

Inactivity. Leaders simply do nothing. They feel so overwhelmed by it all that they shift into ministry neutral. Leaders may think their contributions can accomplish so little. Leaders then wonder, Why do anything at all? Pastors may feel this way because they don't have the power or the influence to implement a mission. The board or powerful people on the board are in charge and may not respect nor value the opinions of their pastors.

3. The Time for a Mission

A characteristic of life today is excessive busyness. Life seems to be passing at breakneck speed, and few believe that they have much discretionary time. Therefore, a valid question is, How much time will it take to develop a mission for your ministry? How much time should you set aside for the crafting process? I have good news for you. When you calculate the time that it takes to develop the "ministry basics" (core values, mission, vision, and strategy) you should discover that the mission consumes the least amount of time.

The reason the mission requires less time than the values, vision, or strategy is because it's shorter and the Scriptures provide the core content for the statement. For example, the Bible dictates the church's mission statement (Matt. 28:19; Mark 16:15). All that's left for the developers is the wording. However, the process of writing and editing the mission statement and achieving a consensus for its ministry-wide adoption rarely happens in a single session. It's a process that most often takes place over three to five sessions, lasting several hours each, and requires some reflective time between sessions.

▼▼▼

The process of developing the mission statement most often takes place over three to five sessions, lasting several hours each, and requires some reflective time between sessions.

▲▲▲

Much depends on the development team and how well they agree on such things as the other ministry basics, particularly the core values that will dictate most of their decisions. If there are problems, most of them will not be theological but philosophical and relational. For some teams, it could become an extremely difficult and time-consuming task where the choice of a single word may arouse intense controversy. I suspect, however, that this would be the exception, not the norm. Regardless, the development of a biblical, functional mission statement is well worth the time and effort because it will serve the organization as an enormously helpful leadership tool with long-term positive impact.

4. The Place for a Mission

Where is the best place to meet when developing a mission statement? The crafting of a significant, biblical mission statement most likely will take several sessions consisting of two to four hours per session. Much depends on prior "think time" and the times of reflection between the major sessions. This means that the team may not find it necessary to use a retreat format at some outside facility. Their own facilities may prove sufficient. There are several advantages to remaining close to home. One is that most believe they don't spend enough time with their families as is. Another is that your own bed provides a better night's sleep.

There are a few disadvantages to this approach. When you remain on-site, the chances that someone will interrupt you are far greater. A zealous secretary or a family member will more quickly interrupt you when you're accessible geographically. Also, there's something emotionally refreshing about new or different surroundings that promotes the creative processes.

Another option is to go away for the day and attempt to complete as much of the process as possible. This would allow for no interruptions and a large chunk of time for intense, creative reflection. In addition, it's more relaxing and refreshing emotionally. One of the departments at Dallas Seminary retreats to a nearby health facility that has rooms available for meetings. After a good day of meeting and work, the team members relax in the sauna, go for a swim, or use the equipment to workout before heading for home.

5. The Cost for a Mission

Next to the time requirements, the most frequent inquiry is the cost of developing a mission statement. If the mission development team uses its present facility, then it incurs no additional expenses. For some, this may be the only option at a time when they are experiencing a shortage of funds.

▼▼▼

The development of a compelling, clear mission statement is too important to let minor costs get in the way.

▲▲▲

If the team decides to retreat to another facility nearby it will incur some additional expenses. Most find, however, that they are minimal. Such added expenses are the cost of renting a room, a meal or two, coffee and refreshments, and any travel expenses such as gasoline. Even these costs can be kept to a minimum (a club sandwich instead of a filet mignon) and should not be allowed to detract from a one day "getaway." The development of a compelling, clear mission statement is too important to let minor costs get in the way.

THE PERSONNEL FOR DEVELOPING A MISSION

Not only must there be the proper preparation for the development of the core mission, but the right people need to be involved in the process. The primary question that I'll address is, Who should write it?

There are several different approaches to developing and writing a mission statement. In some situations, one person develops the entire statement. In other situations, a group may use a team approach. Still others will bring in outside assistance in the process.

Finally, there is a top-down approach where the ministry head, such as a pastor or a seminary president, writes the entire mission and passes it on to the team as unquestioned dogma.

While there is no consensus as to which way works best, someone has to initiate the process. My advice as a leader and ministry consultant is for the senior or point leader to develop and write the initial mission statement, then present it to the board and other staff and lay leaders for review and input, giving the team permission to add to, delete from, or leave it as is. This way everyone gets their "fingerprints" on the mission and, thus, experiences a sense of ownership. This serves to get people on board and to stake a claim in the mission's fulfillment.

The fundamental decisions about such ministry basics as the core mission can be made only at the highest level. This is the responsibility of those who lead at this level—it comes with the territory. The leadership in general and the point person in particular most often is the one with the time, the training, and the desire to define and articulate the ministry's mission. While most people want to have a say in the process, they also want to be led by leaders who they believe are competent and gifted. People want to know that the mission is fully supported by those at the top. If the mission doesn't have leadership support, then it's not likely to materialize.

▼▼▼

People want to know that the mission is fully supported by those at the top. If the mission doesn't have leadership support, then it's not likely to materialize.

▲▲▲

At the same time, the most effective mission statements come from within the heart of the institution—its people. Peter Drucker wisely points out that people determine the performance capacity of an organization. More important, the New Testament teaches the same (Eph. 4; 1 Cor. 12; Rom. 12). Your ministry will be no better than the gifted people who choose to be a part of it. A mission has to be something that both the leaders and the people can share. As many people as possible should participate meaningfully in the process. Let them get their "fingerprints" all over the initial product, especially those in leadership positions within the ministry.

The process is as important as the product. A mission statement created by someone else never possesses the power to inspire commitment and involvement even when you agree with what it says. There's something very important about being a part of the process that makes a world of difference in committing to the product. When you aren't involved in the process but have good leaders, you may vote for the product. But voting in favor of the product and voting to be personally involved aren't the same: you vote with your feet, not with your hands.

In spite of this, there may be some necessary limitations. The size of the ministry will affect people's involvement. The larger a ministry in numbers, the less involvement there will be on a grassroots level. It would be most difficult in a church of several thousand people for the typical member and/or attendee to have much, if any, input. Such an attempt might prove to be more harmful than helpful. It could serve only to neuter a significant, biblical statement. Large churches will rely on the senior pastor, the pastoral staff, the board, and key leaders throughout the church to draft the mission. However, organizations such as large churches will need to have "town hall" meetings at which they present and receive input from the people. In addition, regardless of its polity, a church would be wise to have the congregation vote on something as important as the mission statement.

The smaller church could and probably should solicit input from its members and even its attendees. The downside of this is that it allows the "squeaky wheels" to voice their opinions as well. At the same time, those who are unhappy with the concept or the results will likely acknowledge that they have been heard whether or not their objections or distractions become a part of the final document.

Some ministries will struggle with mission subjectivity. They will discover, on the one hand, that they are too close to their situation to be objective. On the other hand, they know best their ministry situation. A wise move is to develop and write the mission in-house, but use the skills and abilities of an outside consultant. A consultant brings much knowledge and expertise to the process as well as the fresh objectivity of an outsider. The time the consultant will save you and the quality of the final product will more than offset any expenses you might incur. It will also send a strong message about the importance of having a clear, dynamic mission for the ministry.

THE PROCESS FOR DEVELOPING A MISSION

The definition of a mission provided in chapter 2—a broad, brief, biblical statement of what your ministry is supposed to be doing—provides a foundation for the development of your ministry's mission statement and a test for the final product.

The development of your mission statement involves working

through each element in the definition as a distinct step in the process. If you remember the definition of the mission and the elements in particular, then you'll know the process for developing your mission by heart. This section will walk you through the four mission developing steps beginning with the last element and working forward. Each will take the form of a question. I have provided a summary of the process in appendix B to serve both as a guide in the development process and as a test of the final product.

Step 1: What are we supposed to be doing according to the Bible?

We begin with the very last element in the definition. Our definition tells us that a mission is what our ministry is supposed to be doing. In order to figure out what we are supposed to be doing, and thus begin constructing our mission statement, we must combine the last element with the third, which states that the mission is biblical. We must turn to the Scriptures to answer the question: What are we supposed to be doing? No other source will do. God determines our ministry mission, and he reveals this in his Word. In order to complete step number one, you must determine what kind of ministry you are in, who you are trying to serve, and how you are going to serve them.

What kind of ministry are you involved in?

You can separate all Christian ministries into church and parachurch. If you serve in a church ministry, Christ has predetermined your mission. According to Matthew 28:19, Christ's mission for the church is: "Therefore, go and make disciples of all nations." According to Mark 16:15, Christ's mission is: "Go into all the world and preach the good news to all creation." The church's mission has everything to do with pursuing lost people, evangelizing lost people, and then leading them to maturity or Christlikeness. In short—making disciples!

If you serve in a parachurch ministry, Scripture may address what you're supposed to be doing either directly or indirectly. If your ministry centers on evangelism, then you should discover what the Bible teaches about evangelism. If it focuses on moving Christians toward maturity, then you need to know what Scripture teaches about maturity. The same is true for missions' agencies, Christian schools, colleges, seminaries, as well as all the other parachurch ministries.

Whom are you trying to serve?

A ministry's mission is directed at people, not things such as programs. This is because biblical ministry is people-directed. Therefore, we must determine who the recipient of our ministry is to be, who our target audience is. Ultimately, who benefits when we do what we're supposed to be doing?

▼▼▼

A ministry's mission is directed at people,
not things such as programs.

▲▲▲

There are a number of potential recipients. They might be the downtrodden and disenfranchised. They could be churched or unchurched lost people. They might be seekers, Christians, worshippers, students, children, teens, college students, adults, or a certain profession such as teachers, airline pilots, or medical doctors. The target audience could consist of a combination of these people. This would characterize the local church that seeks to win the lost and bring the saved to maturity.

How will your ministry serve people?

A number of businesses have learned that there is a difference between selling a commodity and selling a product. A commodity is usually what the customer walks out with in his or her hand; the product is what he or she feels as they walk out the door. Revlon knows that its not in the cosmetics business. It sells hope. Chanel isn't selling perfume; it's selling fantasy. McDonald's knows that it's not in the fast food business. Its business is entertaining kids and giving their parents a break. Maids, a division of ServiceMaster, doesn't offer its customers a clean house; it offers them peace of mind. The former is a commodity while the latter is a product. The church's commodity—what the customer walks out the door with—is the gospel. The product is transformation—a changed life.

Unlike businesses, churches don't provide commodities, but they do provide a product. What does our ministry offer those within and outside the church? Is it peace of mind, love, closeness to God, compassion, friendship, forgiveness, authentic biblical community, hope, a whole new way of life?

▼▼▼

Unlike businesses, churches don't provide commodities,
but they do provide a product.

▲▲▲

Far too many ministries have not carefully thought through this issue and are focused on things rather than people. They are focused on the means rather than the ends. Christian schools and seminaries focus on teaching biblical facts and content more than on nurturing Christians who can apply the Scriptures to their lives. Somehow in the emphasis to preach the Word, people get left out. While the proclamation of the Word is of paramount importance, it is a means to an end. Some worship leaders work hard at producing good worship rather than good worshippers. Again, worship is important but is the means to the end, not the end in itself. Often Christian publishers focus more on producing good books than on producing biblically literate readers. Biblically literate people who apply the Scriptures to their lives and are worshippers of God are the end. The communication of biblical facts, inspiring worship, and the production of quality Christian literature are all the means to the end, the process to the product, the activities that produce the result, the methods that accomplish the goal.

Pastor Larry Brown and his board settled on a mission statement that satisfies all the above criteria: *The mission of Grace Community Church is to turn both unchurched and churched people into completely committed Christians.* First, it incorporates what the Bible says the church is supposed to be doing—making disciples or "completely committed Christians." Second, it identifies whom the church desires to serve—both lost people and its own saved people. Third, it states specifically what it will do to serve these people—to turn them into "completely committed Christians."

Step 2: Can you articulate your mission in a written statement?

Another element in the definition of a mission is that it is a statement—"a statement of what the ministry is supposed to be doing." It's a written not a verbal statement, so the second step in the mission development process is to write the mission down. The effectiveness of a mission is that when it's written down people can see it, whereas the effectiveness of a vision is in its verbal communication.

▼▼▼

*Writing your mission statement
on a piece of paper forces you to be
disciplined in your thinking.*

▲▲▲

In his excellent book *Learning to Lead*, Fred Smith writes: "In my view, nothing is properly defined until you write it down. Writing forces you to be specific; it takes the fuzz off your thinking."[1] Writing your mission statement on a piece of paper forces you to be disciplined in your thinking. It helps to clarify and focus your thoughts. The only reason that you wouldn't be able to write it down is if you didn't know it. When you know and understand your mission, then you'll be able to articulate it in written form.

This usually involves constantly thinking and rethinking, shaping and reshaping, and drafting and redrafting the mission statement. This is how the leader personalizes his church's mission statement to his congregation. It's highly unusual that anyone articulates the final statement at the first attempt—so be patient with the process.

There are a few things to keep in mind as you begin. You should think about your choice of words, which ones communicate best with your target group. Are they a more traditional group who prefer the old, familiar cliches, or are they a younger, more contemporary group who prefer creative, contemporary terms?

You should also think about clarity to make sure people understand what you're saying. For example, a number of mission statements have substituted words like "fully devoted followers" in place of the term disciple*s* because they believe the former communicates better their concept of discipleship. I'll say more about clarity in the last step.

You must also decide on a format that best conveys your mission. The only limit is your creative ability, but at the risk of stifling that creativity, here are three suggestions. The first looks like this:

The mission of <u>(name of ministry)</u> is to _____
_____.

The advantage of this format is that it's simple and straightforward. However, it is more formal and less personal.

A more personal approach is to place the name of the ministry somewhere above the statement and then express it in the following manner:

Name of Your Ministry
Our mission is to _____.

A third recurring approach is to begin with the name of your ministry and follow it with the words "seeks to."

(Name of your ministry) seeks to _____

_____.

All three examples use the form of an infinitive. If you choose to use this format, then your choice of the exact infinitive depends on what you do for your target audience. Your answer to the question in step 1—How will your ministry serve people?—is the key to the exact infinitive you will use. The following is a list of infinitives others have used that might appear in your mission statement:

to produce	to energize
to equip	to help
to develop	to establish
to assist	to supply
to win	to evangelize
to turn	to encourage
to promote	to transform
to prepare	to create
to provide	to lead
to empower	

Pastor Larry Brown and his board used the first format and the infinitive "to turn": *The mission of Grace Community Church is to turn both unchurched and churched people into completely committed Christians.* They feel that this statement best summarizes how they hope to serve their ministry community. They discussed the choice of the term *committed* because it's such a strong word; they felt it might scare some people away. However, all agreed that they were tired of a maintenance ministry and wanted to call their people to the highest of commitments for Christ.

Step 3: Is the mission statement brief and simple?

The third step in the mission development process is brevity. A mission statement must be brief; this is the second element of the original definition.

The fundamental error most ministries make in mission development is packing too much information into the statement. Mission developers must realize that most people can't effectively process large streams of information and new data. In *The Charismatic Leader*, Jay Conger writes that the average person can handle only six to seven pieces of new data in their short term memory. Consequently, the more information that you include in the mission statement, the greater the likelihood that a person will not comprehend it or remember it. You must resist the temptation to overload your mission statement. The secret to helping people understand and own your mission is brevity and simplicity.

There are several ways that mission developers commit information overload. One is to include the definition of the ministry with the mission statement. Here is an example:

The Ozark Baptist Association

The mission of the Ozark Baptist Association, a community of area churches gathered together under the headship of Christ, is to win the lost and mature the saved.

The statement "a community of area churches gathered under the headship of Christ" defines who the Ozark Baptist Association is. This may or may not be an important statement. However, to include it in the mission statement only serves to detract from the mission. If it's that important, then make it a separate statement.

The Ozark Baptist Association

The Ozark Baptist Association is a community of area churches gathered together under the headship of Christ.

Our mission is to win the lost and mature the saved.

Another way to overload your constituency is to include the strategy for accomplishing the mission along with the mission. Here's an example:

The mission of the Rose Hill Christian Businessmen's Committee is to extend God's kingdom through recruiting Christian business people in the marketplace, training them to share their faith with their business associates, and hosting a nonthreatening weekly meeting where this can take place.

The mission of this fictional organization is found in the first two lines but isn't very clear. The strategy for accomplishing the mission makes up the rest of the statement beginning with the preposition "through." The problem is that the reader will probably miss the mission due to interest in or possible confusion over the strategy.

The statement of strategy is far too important to the ministry to be placed at the end of the mission statement. It deserves a separate statement that is fully developed so that the reader understands precisely how the church or parachurch ministry plans to accomplish the mission. I'll say more about the relationship of the mission and the strategy in chapter 7.

A third way to confuse people is to include the identification of your organization with the statement of mission. Here's an example:

> Oakdale Community Church, a church plant of People's Community Church in Richardson, Texas, desires to transform its people into fully functioning followers of Christ.

Including the identification of the church along with the mission statement isn't a major error, depending on its length. However, note how it breaks up what is an excellent statement and somewhat distracts the reader. This information is necessary as people should know who is involved in planting the church. As in the other examples above, this information should be placed elsewhere in your ministry proposal.

The worst thing that you could do in the mission development process, besides missing the mission entirely or adopting an unbiblical statement, is to combine some or all these errors in one mission statement. We'll look at more of these possible combinations and distractions in the next chapter as we learn how to assess good and poor statements of mission.

The power of your mission statement is found in its brevity and simplicity. Once you have developed the statement, see if it passes the "T-shirt test." If you limit it to a short and simple sentence then you should have no problem fitting it on a T-shirt, no matter how large or small.

In addition, the simpler and shorter the statement, the greater the likelihood that it will be retained. The goal is to provide a mission statement that your people not only understand but remember. The moment you go from one sentence to two or more, you lose the majority of people. The mass of words and sentences overwhelms them. When people see a lot of verbiage, they sense that they'll have to commit too much time to reading and comprehending all the words to make it worthwhile, so they move on to something else. The inclusion of definitions, strategies, identifications, and other words and statements only detract from your mission and ensure that people will not remember it.

Step 4: Is your mission statement broad but clear?

This is the first element of a mission's definition, that it must be broad, and it makes up the fourth step in developing it as a mission statement. In determining what you're supposed to be doing, make sure your answer is the primary, overarching goal of the ministry. It must be central, comprehensive, or all-embracing of what you do to serve people. Therefore, you are looking for an umbrella statement that covers all your ministry bases.

Most organizations have multiple functions. The church, for example, worships, evangelizes, educates, and communicates. The core mission is the task that is at the top of the priority hierarchy. As you write the mission, ask: Is this statement broad enough to cover all that this ministry does or plans to do in the future? What fits under it and what doesn't? On the one hand, if some ministry doesn't fit, then the mission might not be expansive enough. On the other hand, the mission may be correct, and the particular ministry is beyond the scope of the mission. A Christian publishing house, for example, might be operating a soup kitchen somewhere in the inner city. In this case, jettison the ministry—turn it over to another ministry. Otherwise, additional ministries that are outside your mission will diffuse your focus and confuse your constituency.

As you seek breadth in your mission statement, make sure that it remains clear and, thus, understandable. The danger is that the statement can become so broad that it doesn't say or mean anything. The key *clarity* question that you must ask repeatedly of your statement is: What does this mean?

Some mission statements may be regional, that is, they communicate clearly within a certain geographical region but not outside that part of the country. For example, a mission statement in New England might include such terms as *commonwealth, constitution,* and *heritage* that people in other regions might not understand. This is okay as long as you don't attempt to use it in another region that's not as familiar with colonial New England and its early history.

Some churches like to use a statement that includes the term *glory* such as "the glory of God," or "to glorify Christ." While these statements are very biblical, they are so broad that they mask clarity. For the sake of clarity, substitute what glorifying God really means or what your ministry is doing specifically that glorifies God. The same is true for such other words and statements as "to honor God," "to exalt Christ," "to pursue the kingdom of God," and so on—give specifics! Paul reminds us of the importance of clear communication in 1 Corinthians 14:8: "Again, if the trumpet does not sound a clear call, who will get ready for battle?"

▼▼▼

The crucial test of mission clarity is the "people-test."

▲▲▲

The crucial test of mission clarity is the "people-test." As you develop your mission statement, ask various people what it means to them. Quiz people within your organization. If it's a church, then ask board members, secretaries, even visitors to tell you what the statement communicates to them. Though the mission statement is primarily "in house"—for the people who have committed to your ministry— consider quizzing people outside the organization. If they don't understand it, then it may be too broad. If all understand it, then you have a broad but clear mission statement that communicates.

The board of Grace Community Church knew that their new mission statement was broad and clear—it had passed the "people-test." They had quizzed a number of their congregants from attenders to lay leaders, and found that most seemed to grasp and like their final statement. They had cleared a crucial hurdle because other matters in the past had been met with opposition. The board sensed that God was working with their people, and there now existed a new spirit within the congregation.

They also knew that they had a lot of work ahead in bringing their ministry in-line with the new mission. While it was broad enough to cover a number of their ministries, approximately a third didn't fit. The church had been in existence for thirty years and had added a number of programs, many of which were now defunct and clearly beyond the mission of the church. However, no one had the heart to discontinue them. They were like numerous coats of paint, and the bottom layer had begun to peel, affecting the rest. All this would change—it was time to scrape off the excess paint.

QUESTIONS FOR THOUGHT AND DISCUSSION

1. Is the leadership convinced that your ministry needs a clear, dynamic mission? If yes, how do you know? If no, why? Who is convinced, and who isn't?

2. Would the mission audit help convince your ministry leaders of the need for a mission? If no, why not? Would you use the audit with your people? Why or why not?

3. Is your ministry ready to develop a mission? If your answer is no, is it because of any of the three barriers (exception,

procrastination, inactivity) mentioned in this chapter? If yes, which one(s)? If no, then why?

4. How much time should you set aside for the mission development process? How much time have you set aside? Do you anticipate any problems that might delay the process? If yes, what are they?

5. Have you decided where the mission development team will meet? How much do you estimate that the process will cost? Do you have the necessary funds?

6. Who will and who should write your mission statement? Who is responsible for initiating and pursuing the process? Who will be allowed to get their "fingerprints" all over the mission statement? Who decides who's involved?

7. How many people are involved in your ministry? How will the size of your ministry affect who is involved in the development process? Do you believe that the process is as important as the product? Explain.

8. Do you believe that the information on mission development is or will be helpful to you and your mission development team? Why or why not? Is there anything that you didn't find helpful or would add to the process?

9. If you've already developed a mission statement, did you use the mission development process as a test of a good mission statement? If yes, did it prove helpful?

ENDNOTE

1. Fred Smith, *Learning to Lead* (Waco, Tex.: Word Books, 1986), 34.

5

The Development of the Mission
Part 2: The Test of a Good Mission Statement

Those who were a key part of the mission development team at Grace Community Church were surprised at how
quickly they came up with what they unanimously agreed was a
mission statement tailor-made for their church. What they learned
later was that Pastor Larry Brown had a head start. On the one hand,
he had already developed the mission statement that with a few
tweaks the board and the church adopted as theirs. On the other
hand, he knew the mission development process and used it both to
develop and test Grace Community's mission.

Later Pastor Larry told one of the board members that the mission seminar at the leadership conference had helped him im-
mensely to understand the mission concept by testing or evaluating
both good and poor mission statements from church and parachurch
organizations as well as from the marketplace. The professor who
led the seminar placed these mission statements on an overhead
projector and asked the attendees to evaluate each based on the four
step mission development process. He initiated the process, but it
didn't take long before the attendees caught on and made some
excellent observations on their own.

This chapter presents the fourth *p:* the product of the mission. The
process concludes with a product—the mission statement itself. In
this chapter, I'll follow the professors example and present and then
test or critique a variety of mission statements, using the mission
development process and its structure from chapter 4.

The development process helps leaders construct a dynamic
mission statement in two ways. First, it provides the process that
produces the product, and then it uses that process to test the product.

Once a ministry has developed its mission statement, it should hold it up to the light of the development process to discover if it's a good one. The product is evaluated using the process. This lets you make needed corrections that also help in crafting a well written, dynamic mission statement. The process serves as a test for older, established mission statements as well. The question in either case is: Does your mission pass muster? Does it pass the test for a good mission statement?

Step 1: What are we supposed to be doing according to the Bible?

In this step and all that follow, I'll use a number of actual mission statements that, in my role as a consultant, I have collected from various sources. They are either good, bad, or somewhere in between. Consequently, I've changed or disguised the bad and in-between ones so as not to hurt or offend their developers. Some of the following mission statements pass the test and some don't. While you can learn what not to do from poor statements, you also need to learn what to do from good statements. There are three mini-questions that, when carefully addressed, will help you to answer the above question posed in step 1.

What kind of ministry are you involved in?

The answer to this question is either a church or parachurch ministry. The purpose of the question is to demonstrate that Christ has predetermined the church's mission in the Scriptures and limited the parachurch's mission to the same. Grace Community Bible Church in Richmond, Texas, provides us with a good example that meets this test:

> The mission of Grace Community Bible Church is to lead the people of northern Fort Bend County to salvation in Jesus Christ and growth in Christlikeness through a dedicated, innovative, and equipped body of gifted people.

The mission of Christ's church is to make disciples (Matt. 28:19; Mark 16:15). This involves moving people from wherever they are (lost or saved) to where God wants them to be (mature or Christlike). The statement "to lead the people of northern Fort Bend County to salvation in Jesus Christ and growth in Christlikeness" fully meets this criterion.

However, some church mission statements aren't clear in this regard. Here is one that is not:

The mission of the Church of Sandy Springs is to provide an environment where people can discover a passion for God that is real and relational.

Since this is a church ministry, you must ask: Where is the Great Commission? Is this what the church is supposed to be doing according to the Scriptures? The answer could be yes. The problem is that you don't know what it means "to provide an environment where people can discover a passion for God that is real and relational."

Whom are you trying to serve?

The purpose of this question is to focus on the ministry's target group. If the organization doesn't know whom they're trying to reach, then chances are very good that they won't reach them or anyone else. Some say that they aren't trying to reach anyone in particular but everyone in general. The result of this approach is that they reach no one at all.

The first example, the one above from Grace Community Bible Church in Richmond, Texas, does an excellent job of identifying its target audience. They are "the people of northern Fort Bend County," an area not too far from Houston, Texas. While it's not necessary to be that specific, you do need to be more focused than the second example from Sandy Springs that refers only to "people." To whom is the statement referring? Are they the people in and around the fictional Sandy Springs community? Are they churched or unchurched, lost or saved? We need to know more about them as in the following:

Our mission is to share the love of God with the people of the mid-cities and beyond so that they can become fully devoted followers of Christ.

Smith Road Baptist Church

This fictional church is more specific for it has targeted "the people of the mid-cities and beyond." While we, who aren't from the area, don't know where the "mid-cities" are located, the people of the church do. However, the church could be a little clearer about its mission—what does it mean "to share the love of God?"

Another statement that identifies well its target group is the following:

> The mission of Lawrence Bible Church is to share the impact of God's love so that seekers and believers can reach their full potential in Christ.

Those who are a part of Lawrence Bible Church know that their target audience is both seekers (the lost) and believers. They are the target of the Great Commission. However, the statement "to share the impact of God's love" is a little ambiguous.

A final statement that does an excellent job of identifying its target people is that of Mission to the Americas, a church planting mission located in Wheaton, Illinois.

> In obedience to Jesus Christ, OUR MISSION is to evangelize, disciple, and congregationalize the unreached of the Americas, including the disenfranchised and ethnically diverse people.

Is there any question as to whom they are targeting? If you were a potential church planter who was considering joining Mission to the Americas, would you have any doubt as to whom the mission is attempting to reach? That's the advantage of clearly designating your target audience in the mission statement.

How will your ministry serve people?

This third question forces the church or parachurch ministry to look at what it plans to do for people, whether saved or lost, churched or unchurched, from a biblical perspective. It is also a reminder that ministries are in the "people business." They are here to reach and serve people.

The first example from Grace Community Bible Church is quite clear about how they will serve people. Here, again, is their mission statement:

> The mission of Grace Community Bible Church is to lead the people of northern Fort Bend County to salvation in Jesus Christ and growth in Christlikeness through a dedicated, innovative, and equipped body of gifted people.

Grace's mission is to lead the lost in their target audience to salvation in Jesus Christ and help them and others to grow in Christlikeness. This is a biblical mission statement that signals what will happen to you if you live in their part of the county and respond to their ministry. The only problem with it is the last phrase. I'll say more about it later in this chapter.

Another good biblical statement is the mission of Crossroads Church, a potential church plant in the McKinney, Texas, an area located north of Dallas, Texas.

> The mission of Crossroads Church is to convert the lost and build up nominal believers into committed followers of Jesus Christ.

Its mission is twofold and in perfect alignment with Christ's Great Commission. First, it serves the lost outside the church by converting them. Second, it serves nominal believers by building them into committed followers of Jesus Christ. This is a nice balance between what the church does for the lost who are outside the body and the saved who most likely are within the body. The church's poignant mission is to target and serve both groups.

A third example that's not so good is that of the church of Sandy Springs mentioned above. I'll repeat it so that you don't have to turn back to it.

> The mission of the Church of Sandy Springs is to provide an environment where people can discover a passion for God that is real and relational.

One of the problems here is that you don't know for certain how the church serves people. What does providing "an environment where people can discover a passion for God that is real and relational" mean? Frankly, it sounds great, and I would love to serve in a church that does this. I desire with all my heart that my passion for God be real and relational. Only I'm not sure what that is. A more important question is: Do the people in this church know what it means?

Here's another ambiguous example.

> Our church is united around a common mission of doing something significant with our lives—to invest them totally in the kingdom of God.

> Southshore Church

Like the example above it, this one sounds very good. I want to be a part of a group of Christians who are united around a common mission. I, too, want to do something significant with my life, and I sincerely want to invest my life totally in the kingdom of God.

The problem is that I don't know what that is, or at least what it means to this church. I'm confused whether this is biblical—I think it is—and how it will serve people.

Step 2: Can you articulate your mission in a written statement?

The goal in step 2 is to get the mission down on paper—to put it in the form of a statement. Writing it helps to clarify your thinking and focus your thoughts. It blows any mental dust off your mind; it clears away the cognitive cobwebs. Step 2 asks three mini-questions.

What words communicate best with your target group?

It's imperative that your ministry understand its target group. This involves both demographics and psychographics. From a business perspective, demographics tell you who your customers are, and psychographics tell you *why* they buy what they buy. From a ministry perspective, the first reveals who your target group is and provides such information as their education, income, marital status, and other similar facts. The second tells you why they behave the way they do and addresses their needs, wants, desires, and so on. Doing your demographic and psychographic homework will aid you in selecting the precise words that will communicate best with your target audience whoever they are and wherever they live.

Some terms are regional and limited to a particular part of the country. In chapter 4, I mentioned terms that are regional to the Northeast. Here is a mission statement for Colonial Chapel, a church located somewhere in Connecticut.

> Our mission is to colonize Connecticut and the greater commonwealth with citizens of Heaven who possess a new spiritual constitution, who passionately embrace the revolutionary teachings of Jesus Christ, who have declared themselves "in dependence" upon God, His word and His people, and whose mission is to proclaim the truth which sets men free, liberating them from the rule of darkness.

It's obvious that the mission developers didn't produce this regional statement in one sitting. Its creativity reflects much thinking and rethinking, drafting and redrafting. Most in America are quick to realize that this is a statement for a ministry in New England. It would seem "out of place" in any other part of the country. People who live in New England, and particularly those who live in

Connecticut, are more familiar than the rest of us with such terms as commonwealth, constitution, and revolutionary.

Do your people understand what you've written?

People may be from the same region, but that doesn't necessarily mean that they understand the terms that you include in your mission statement. According to a Gallup poll a large number of Americans are biblically illiterate. Thus, they may not understand the biblical terms that you might use such as *disciple*. In fact, there is confusion over the meaning of this term among Christians who are biblically literate.

Consequently, you may want to substitute a few words of explanation in place of a term like *disciple*. Along with teaching at Dallas Theological Seminary, I pastor Northwood Community Church in Dallas, Texas. The following is our mission statement:

> The mission of Northwood Community Church is to be used of God in developing people into fully functioning followers of Christ.

We asked, What is a disciple? Our answer is "a fully functioning follower of Christ." We explain that fully functioning followers of Christ at Northwood are characterized by the three cs: conversion, commitment, and contribution. They have been converted to Christ, committed their lives to Christ, and are contributing to Christ. Our strategy builds directly on these three characteristics.

Another example is the mission of Willow Creek Community Church in South Barrington, near Chicago, Illinois.

> The mission of Willow Creek Community Church is to turn irreligious people into fully devoted followers of Jesus Christ.[1]

It would appear that Willow Creek wrestled with what the term *disciple* communicated to its people. Rather than using that term, they substituted the words "fully devoted followers." Obviously they believed that this—devotion to Christ—communicated best what discipleship should mean for them and their target audience.

Another similar example is the statement of Pantego Bible Church in Arlington, Texas.

> Our mission is to transform people, through the work of the Holy Spirit, into fully developing followers of Christ.[2]

The pastor, Randy Frazee, writes: "Other churches have similar statements. When we developed the statement, we knew it sounded familiar, but we couldn't place it. Months later, we uncovered a popular church that had a statement that is almost identical."[3] Regardless the source, Frazee felt that the words "fully developing followers" communicated precisely what they meant to their target audience—the people of Arlington. They are more intent on "developing followers" than on "fully devoted followers." While the difference may seem trivial, it could make all the difference in reaching your ministry's target group.

Does your format convey well your mission?

How you express your mission statement or the form that it takes allows much room for creativity. The actual form, itself, isn't that important. What is important is that the form you use clearly communicates your mission to your target people. You want them to "get it."

Most of the mission statements in my collection use one of two forms. The first is the format of Crossroads Church mentioned above.

> The mission of Crossroads Church is to convert the lost and build up nominal believers into committed followers of Jesus Christ.

Crossroads' mission statement fits the following format:

> The mission of (<u>name of your ministry</u>) is to _____ _____.

There are several advantages to this format. It's simple, clear, and gets straight to the point. No one is left wondering what the mission statement is—it tells you outright. The disadvantage is that it seems a little formal and less personal. Regardless, if you like this approach, then all you need to do is place the name of your ministry in the space provided and add your mission.

The second form usually presents the name of the church somewhere else or places it immediately above the statement. Regardless, the reader knows the identity of the organization. If Crossroads Church used this format, it would look like the following:

Crossroads Church

> Our mission is to convert the lost and build up nominal believers into committed followers of Jesus Christ.

The format looks like this:

Name of the Organization

Our mission is to _____

_____.

This format has all the advantages of the former—simple, clear, gets to the point—but it includes a less formal, more personal approach with the use of the personal pronoun "our" at the very beginning of the statement. If you prefer this, then all you need do is place your mission in the space provided.

A third form is the one prepared by the fictional Jonesville Church that is located somewhere in your community.

Jonesville Church seeks to do whatever it takes to bring as many people as possible to faith in Christ and membership in the church.

This format looks like this:

(Name of your ministry) seeks to _____

_____.

The only disadvantage of this form is that the statement doesn't signal to the reader that this is the church's mission statement. After you read it, you might have to pause mentally and ask: Was this it? Did I miss it? Do I need to keep on reading? You could easily correct this by placing the words "Mission Statement" above the statement. Other verbs could be used in place of "seeks" such as "desires," "aspires," "lives," and so on.

A problematic format is that of the fictional Colleyville Community Church.

Colleyville Community Church exists to provide a caring and nurturing environment for people of faith.

Not only does the statement fail to reflect the Great Commission (it sounds more like a Christian retirement home), but it uses the verb "exists." This verb implies purpose. In effect, it says that the purpose of Colleyville Community Church is to provide a caring and nurturing environment. The problem is that the mission and the purpose of an organization are different. According to chapter 2, the purpose of the church, or the reason it exists, is much broader—to glorify Christ. The mission serves a different function entirely. Therefore, this is a purpose statement, not a mission statement.

This sense of purpose is even more evident for a number of churches who have adopted a similar mission statement:

> Our church exists to glorify God by making disciples who love God, love one another, and love people who are lost.

As in the prior example, the term *exists* signals that this is a purpose statement. It's followed by the theological purpose of the church—to glorify God (Pss. 22:23; 50:15; Rom. 15:6; 1 Cor. 6:20).

One part of speech that all the above examples have in common is an infinitive immediately after the main verb. Turn to page 72 for a list of infinitives that I have observed and collected from various mission statements. The list might help you in selecting and articulating the precise infinitive for your mission statement.

Step 3: Is the mission statement brief and simple?

The third step focuses on brevity and simplicity. Long mission statements are hard to remember, and the power of a compelling mission statement is in its simplicity. Step 3 poses four mini-questions.

Have you committed information overload?

You must resist the temptation to pack as much information as is possible in your mission statement. Remember that people can't and won't process a large amount of data.

Information overload occurs when the definition of the organization is included along with its mission. The definition answers the *who* question: As a ministry, who are you? The mission answers the *what* question: What do you do? When mission developers combine the two, they confuse who the organization is with what it does. While some may discern the difference, it's confusing to the average layperson. If you feel that it's important to include the definition of your organization, then keep it separate from the mission statement for reasons of clarity.

The following provide several examples that combine the definition with the mission. The first is for a church ministry.

> Faith Community Church is a contemporary community composed of Christian men and women who want to have an impact on eternity. We are convinced that our comprehensive mission is to win the lost in our part of the metroplex to Christ.

The opening sentence supplies a descriptive definition for Faith Community Church. The verb "is" signals that a definition might follow, and we're not disappointed. The second sentence presents the actual mission statement that focuses on evangelism. The definition seems to be important and probably merits special attention. However, for the sake of clarity, it should be included in a separate paragraph.

Another example from a parachurch ministry is the mission statement for the Center for Biblical and Theological Studies—a ministry within a divinity school.

> The Center for Biblical and Theological Studies, a ministry of Smith Divinity School, is committed to developing scholars to advance the cause of academics in higher Christian education.

The statement "a ministry of Smith Divinity School," though separated by commas, serves to define and identify the Center for Biblical and Theological Studies. You could rewrite it so that it's similar in form to that of Faith Community Church.

> The Center for Biblical and Theological Studies is a ministry of Smith Divinity School. Its mission is to develop scholars who advance the cause of academics in higher Christian education.

Regardless of how you rewrite it, the mission developer must decide how important the definition is. The authors of the above examples must have felt that definitions were important, or they wouldn't have included them with their mission statements. If you determine that your definition is not that important, then drop it from the statement. If it's important, include it in a separate statement. This will serve to emphasize its importance along with but separate from the mission statement.

Information overload also occurs when a statement of means or strategy is included along with the ministry's mission. The problem is that while the mission answers the *what* question, the means answers the *how* question: How will the ministry accomplish its mission? Both are vital to a ministry, but must be kept separate to avoid confusing the two.

Including the strategy or means with the mission is the most common error that I encounter in studying and developing church and parachurch mission statements. This takes place in a variety of formats.

A subtle example is found in the statement of the fictional Haskell Avenue Community Church.

> Our mission is to share God's love with all the people in our community in creative ways that will help them become Christ's disciples.

The phrase "in creative ways" is a statement of means, not mission. It's describing how the church will share God's love with all the people in their community. So what? Though seemingly minuscule in significance, nevertheless, it adds an element of confusion to the mission statement. Therefore, in the interest of clarity, I would urge that it be left out.

Another example is the excellent statement of Grace Community Bible Church near Houston, Texas.

> The mission of Grace Community Bible Church is to lead the people of northern Fort Bend County to salvation in Jesus Christ and growth in Christlikeness through a dedicated, innovative, and equipped body of gifted people.

The mission statement actually ends with the term *Christlikeness*. The rest of the sentence relates the means or strategy to accomplish this mission—"through a dedicated, innovative, and equipped body of gifted people." The mission statement would be even clearer if the means were moved to a separate statement or dropped altogether.

A final example is the statement of Willowbend Church:

> The mission of Willowbend Church is to make disciples in the Greater Minneapolis area through creative, Christ honoring worship; teaching that is biblical and relevant to life; vital, supportive community groups; and evangelistic outreach at home and abroad.

The mission statement ends with "area," and the means or strategy for accomplishing this mission begins with the preposition "through" and extends to the end of the sentence. In this example, the strategy is longer than the mission and detracts from its impact. The reader could miss the mission entirely and spend most of his or her time thinking about the strategy. This looks like an excellent strategy, but it should be communicated in a separate strategy statement.

Another example of information overload is when both a definition and a strategy are included with the mission. Of all the ways to overload people with information, this is the most confusing. You can see this in the following statement from the catalog of Transylvania Divinity School.

> The mission of Transylvania Divinity School as a profes-sional, graduate-level school is to prepare men and women for ministry as godly servant-leaders in the body of Christ worldwide. By blending instruction in the Scriptures from our doctrinal perspective with training in ministry skills, the school seeks to produce graduates who do the work of evan-gelism, edify believers, and equip others by proclaiming and applying God's Word in the power of the Holy Spirit.

A descriptive definition is found immediately after the name of the institution—"as a professional, graduate-level school." The state-ment could just as easily read: "Transylvania Divinity School is a professional, graduate-level school." Since the statement is in the school's catalog, most would understand that it's a professional, graduate-level school. It isn't necessary here, especially in a state-ment as long as this one.

The actual mission surrounds the descriptive definition. I've placed the latter in parenthesis. "The mission of Transylvania Divinity School (as a professional graduate-level school) is to prepare men and women for ministry as godly servant-leaders in the body of Christ worldwide."

If the statement stopped here it would be a good one. However, it's followed by a second mission statement: ". . . the school seeks to produce graduates who do the work of evangelism, edify believers, and equip others . . ." And this statement is surrounded by two state-ments of means, each signaled with the preposition "by." All this clutter serves only to leave the reader extremely confused.

Does your statement pass the "T-shirt test?"

I stated in chapter 2 that Peter Drucker says that a good mission state-ment should be short enough to fit on a T-shirt. A fully functional, dy-namic mission statement gains its power from being short and simple.

An example of one that is too long is that above from Transylvania Divinity School. Again, had it stopped after the first mission statement, it would have been a good one. And it would be even better if an editor removed the descriptive definition and placed it somewhere else in the catalog.

Another example is the statement of Faith Community Bible Church.

Our mission is to mobilize our people to accomplish Christ's Great Commission Mandate by equipping believers who love him dearly, who relate authentically in their community groups, and who discover and exercise their ministry gifts to reach unchurched people within their personal spheres of influence such as their work, neighborhoods, communities, and ultimately the entire world.

This isn't as long as Transylvania's mission statement. However, it's one long confusing sentence, whereas, the divinity school's is divided into two sentences. Neither statement would pass Drucker's "T-shirt test," even if the shirt were a double extra-large.

Can you express your mission in one sentence?

The best, most powerful mission statements are one sentence in length. Note the following examples. The first is that of Willow Creek Community Church: "The mission of Willow Creek Community Church is to turn irreligious people into fully devoted followers of Jesus Christ."[4] Note that this is succinct and gets right to the point. The drafters don't fall into the trap of trying to cram too much information into the statement, thus confusing their people.

A second is the mission statement of the Salvation Army. Our mission is ". . . to make citizens out of the rejected."[5] Again, brevity is the power of this mission. There's no question what the Army thinks that it's supposed to be doing. People who come on board know what they're getting into—what lies ahead.

A third is the statement of the Philadelphia Seeker Project, which is an excellent church planting venture led by Dr. Bruce Carter near Philadelphia, Pennsylvania. Their mission is ". . . to establish biblical communities that help seekers become fully devoted followers of Jesus Christ." Actually, the first infinitive is a statement of means that is followed by the mission statement. The mission is: "To help seekers become fully devoted followers of Jesus Christ." The means for accomplishing this is "to establish biblical communities." Regardless, Dr. Carter's entire statement is short, compelling, and gets to the point.

Is your mission memorable?

Above all, people should be able to remember and even articulate your mission statement. A short, dynamic, one-sentence statement that passes the "T-shirt test" is most memorable. The examples above make the point well.

Willow Creek's mission statement—"to turn irreligious people into fully devoted followers"—is easily remembered. The entire statement and the choice of words all join to make for a memorable mission. Once you've heard it, most likely you'll remember it. If you hear it several times, then you've "got it."

The same is true of the Philadelphia Seeker Project's statement—"to help seekers become fully devoted followers of Jesus Christ." This too is most memorable. That it's short and well-worded causes it to stick to your mental ribs.

However, because one sentence statements are memorable, you must resist the temptation to load them down with information. Remember—they're short, one-sentence statements. You'll note that a number of the poor examples cited in this chapter where lengthy, one sentence statements. Here is an example from the fictional Apple Grove Memorial Church:

> The mission of Apple Grove Memorial Church is through the power of the Holy Spirit and through vibrant, uplifting worship to glorify God by becoming a healing body of committed Christians who intentionally win the lost and make disciples, while being committed to do whatever it takes to accommodate growth and plant sister churches in our community and beyond to Christ's glory.

Read this statement one more time. Now turn your head away or close your eyes, and see if you remember it. Try it again. It's only one sentence—why can't you remember it? This is simply another example of information overload that needlessly discourages people from remembering and ultimately owning the statement.

Step 4: Is your mission statement broad but clear?

This final step holds two elements in dynamic tension. You want to land somewhere between the two. The first is breadth, and the second is clarity.

Is your statement broad enough?

The mission statement must be broad enough to include all that your ministry does to serve people. Westbridge Church of West Des Moines, Iowa, accomplishes this in the following:

> Westbridge Church seeks to assist as many people as possible in becoming fully devoted followers of Jesus Christ by being a culturally accessible church for our generation.

Pantego Bible Church in Arlington, Texas, has crafted a statement that is also expansive enough to cover all its ministries.

> Our mission is to transform people, through the work of the Holy Spirit, into fully developing followers of Christ.[6]

The same is true of Grace Community Bible Church of Richmond, Texas:

> The mission of Grace Community Bible Church is to lead the people of northern Fort Bend County to salvation in Jesus Christ and growth in Christlikeness through a dedicated, innovative, and equipped body of gifted people.

What all these statements have in common that accounts for their breadth is the Great Commission. They all touch in different but similar ways Christ's command to make disciples—to move people from prebirth to maturity.

The mission statement of Jonesboro Community Bible Church, however, is not broad enough.

> Our mission is to teach the Scriptures so well that people will hunger and thirst after God's righteousness.

What is the problem? Like so many teaching churches, Jonesboro has missed the Great Commission. It emphasizes teaching the Bible; that is important but is only an aspect of edification. The problem is that it leaves out other critical areas of edification such as worship, and it completely misses evangelism.

Is your statement clear?

On the one hand, the statement must be expansive like those above. On the other hand, statements that use phrases such as "to glorify" God, or Christ, are so broad that they are not clear.

> Our mission is to glorify God by responding to the Savior through exalting him as Lord, edifying his church, and evangelizing his world.

Again, the use of the words "to glorify God" raises the question: What does that mean? Not only is this the purpose of the church, but it's so broad that it goes beyond the church. The rest of the phrases in this statement help to narrow the concept somewhat. However, they raise additional questions: What does exalting Christ mean? What does edifying the church mean?

Another statement that is too broad is the following:

> The mission of Sioux Falls Church is to create an environment in which all people can discover and develop a love for the Savior that is relevant and relational.

This is so broad that it leaves the reader wondering what it's all about. If this is the Great Commission, then it's not obvious. It's most important that we love the Savior. It sounds great but is so expansive as to have lost any clarity for the reader.

The four steps for developing your mission statement above are spread out over a number of pages. To facilitate the development process and to save you time, I have placed the four steps on one page in appendix B.

ENDNOTES

1. Mary Ann Jeffries, "A Variety of Visions," *Leadership*, 15, no. 3 (summer 1994): 35.
2. Randy Frazee with Lyle E. Schaller, *The Comeback Congregation* (Nashville: Abingdon Press, 1995), 61.
3. Ibid.
4. Jeffries, "A Variety of Visions," 35.
5. Peter F. Drucker, *Managing the Non-Profit Organization* (New York: Harper Business, 1990), 4.
6. Frazee with Schaller, *The Comeback Congregation*, 61.

The Communication of the Mission
Nine Ways to Propagate Your Mission

Grace Community Church was congregational in its polity—the people in the pew were used to having a say in what took place in the church. Over the years, they had become accustomed to voting on everything, "including the color of the toilet paper," Pastor Larry would add. While he understood the need for congregational involvement, he believed that it was only necessary for certain key decisions such as the call of a new pastor, the approval of the budget, and a decision to move and rebuild. He believed that churches that voted on everything distrusted their leadership. One such decision, however, was the church's mission; he and the board agreed to bring the final product to the congregation for a vote. The people must support it or it was meaningless. The result was a unanimous decision in favor of the mission. The people were excited about what they heard. Perhaps it signaled a new beginning for the flock.

Pastor Larry was concerned, however, with an attitude that he sensed was spreading among his board members. Now that they had developed and adopted the new mission statement for Grace Community Church, they felt that they could relax—they had arrived. Pastor Larry knew from the mission seminar that there was still much work to accomplish, and he desperately needed the board's help if the church was to ultimately realize its mission. However, congregational and board acceptance of the mission is not enough.

Several critical steps remain if Grace Community is to begin to realize its core, definitive mission. One is the communication of the mission to the ministry community and the ministry constituency. In 1 Corinthians 14:8, Paul warns: "Again, if the trumpet does not sound a clear call, who will get ready for battle?" While the congregation had enthusiastically endorsed the mission, Larry realized that a number of the people didn't really understand what it was all about. Peter Drucker warns: "A nonprofit institution will start to flounder almost immediately unless it clearly defines its mission and emphasizes that mission again and again. This is doubly true for the nonprofit that relies on donors, volunteers, or both."[1]

The mission statement must be emphasized by the pastor and board again and again. Don't confuse this with the casting of the vision. The casting of the vision and the propagation of the mission are similar but different processes.[2] Casting a vision is more a verbal process, whereas propagating a mission is more a visual process. This chapter is the start, not the end, of what is to be the ongoing process of mission propagation. You always should be looking for new, unique ways to keep the mission physically present before your people. Here are nine practical ideas that will help you begin the process.

1. THE LEADERS' LIVES

The leaders' lives communicate the mission by modeling the mission. Leaders must live the mission or risk losing all credibility in their people's eyes. To incarnate the mission, however, they must first own it. This means that each leader has so embraced the mission as to have made a strong personal commitment to it. This is evident when they believe in it to the point that they are willing to act on it.

▼▼▼

The leaders' lives communicate the mission
by modeling the mission.

▲▲▲

The apostle Paul exemplified this kind of leadership commitment to a mission. He supplies a glimpse of his mission in Romans 15:20: "It has always been my ambition to preach the gospel where Christ was not known, so that I would not be building on someone else's foundation." Then in verses 17–19 he relates his personal commitment to accomplish his mission:

> Therefore I glory in Christ Jesus in my service to God. I will not venture to speak of anything except what Christ has accomplished through me in leading the Gentiles to obey God

by what I have said and done—by the power of signs and miracles, through the power of the Spirit. So from Jerusalem all the way around to Illyricum, I have fully proclaimed the gospel of Christ.

The Savior has predetermined the church's mission. It's the Great Commission that consists of making disciples (Matt. 28:19–20; Mark 16:15; Acts 1:8). This may be problematic for some. For example, a pastor may have a different mission for the church than does Christ. He may want to turn it into a teaching church or an evangelistic church. However, the Great Commission includes both of these and more. The pastor in these situations might want to consider another ministry such as teaching in a seminary or working with an evangelistic parachurch organization.

The life and ministry of the leader of a teaching-only church or an evangelism-only church contradicts Christ's mission mandate. The Great Commission includes winning lost people to faith in Christ, but the teaching-church pastor tends to ignore this. In a similar way, the Commission includes relevant Bible teaching, but the evangelist pastor tends to ignore this. Followers constantly observe the lives of their leaders. To them what the leader emphasizes is important, and what he ignores isn't deemed important.

2. FRAMED STATEMENT OR WALL PLAQUE

While staying at a Drury Inn in Colorado Springs, Colorado, I noticed the company's mission statement every time I entered the elevator to go to my room. They had framed and placed it in the elevator above the buttons for each floor. Some hotels place their mission statement on a plaque and mount it on the wall behind the desk where customers check in. The International Bible Society, also located in Colorado Springs, Colorado, took this concept one step further. They have placed their mission statement on a wall in the foyer with letters cut out of wood. As you walk into the building, their mission statement has a way of jumping out at you—you can't miss it, and neither can their employees and volunteers. It's very attractive and well done.

Pastors or parachurch leaders could propagate the ministry's mission by hanging it on the wall in their offices. Their staff could reinforce this by setting framed mission statements on their desks. Placing it on the wall in wood-cut letters would be even more effective and would send an even stronger message. The more effort and the greater the cost expended to display the mission statement, the more impact the mission will have on your people.

3. WALLET-SIZE CARDS

Companies such as Goodyear, Motorola, and Kellogg have placed their mission statements on wallet-size cards. Some have two versions: one to carry and one to have in or on the desk or hanging on the wall. The employees at Motorola use the card for impromptu challenges and games.[3]

The church I pastor, Northwood Community Church in Dallas, Texas, also uses wallet-size cards to propagate our mission statement: "Our mission is to be used of God in developing people into fully functioning followers of Christ" (figure 6.1). The church makes these cards available to our people in hopes that they'll remember, live, and communicate the mission. We expect the congregation to have these cards somewhere on their persons most of the time. Men can keep them in their wallets; women can carry them in their purses. While this may appear extreme, it communicates to the congregation how important their mission really is.

NORTHWOOD COMMUNITY CHURCH

Our mission is to be used of God in developing people into fully functioning followers of Christ.

Figure 6.1

4. VIDEO PRESENTATION

A number of businesses such as Delta Airlines and Gillette have produced video presentations that focus on their corporate mission. The advantage of this method is that it combines an audio as well as a visual approach to communicating the mission. While the mission is best propagated visually, adding an audio dimension serves to reinforce its ultimate effect.

The videotape is an easy, relatively inexpensive way to propagate a church or parachurch's mission. I have noted that more and more parachurch mission agencies have turned to this method. If you're interested in a particular mission organization, and you write them requesting more information, you may receive a videotape through the mail along with a letter or brochure. These tapes are not only informational, seeking to introduce a possible candidate to the mission, but they may include the mission statement. While not formally asking that it be returned, the mission could include a self-addressed, stamped pouch or container that would encourage the potential candidate to mail the videotape back to the mission, making it possible to use the videotape repeatedly.

A church could provide a videotape for its membership and for people who express interest in the church. Members could be encouraged to give it to prospective members or interested neighbors. One of my former students, Thomas Buck, who pastors Westside Baptist Church in New Port Richey, Florida, produced a video containing his church's mission, vision, and values, and the offering increased dramatically.

5. CLASS

Another good opportunity to convey the mission statement is through a class. Some businesses teach courses on their missions. Others pay their employees to attend mission propagation sessions. Both underline in the employee's mind the importance of the statement.

This method can be used just as effectively in both church and parachurch ministries. Most churches conduct new members' classes that consist of reviewing the church's doctrinal statement, constitution, and history. While these things are important, it's sometimes enough to put even the most aspiring new member asleep.

Including time to propagate the church's core mission as well as its vision, core values, and strategy is a better approach. Let people know what the church is prepared to do for them, what it expects of them, how they fit in, and why the church does what it does (its programs).

6. T-SHIRT

If the mission should be short enough to put on a T-shirt, then why not put it on a T-shirt? All kinds of organizations have caught on to using T-shirts to promote their messages as well as their products.

What is amazing is that while some give these shirts away, most sell them. Consequently, individuals pay a particular business for the privilege of advertising that business or its products. It's ingenious. I have found myself in a situation where a business has offered to sell me a T-shirt that advertised it or its product. In jest, I've responded that I'm not interested in purchasing their shirt, however, if they would pay me, then I would wear the shirt and advertise their product. So far, I've had no takers.

A church or parachurch ministry could promote their mission using a T-shirt and increase member unity while generating outside interest. The ministry could place the mission statement on the front or the back, or it could start it on the front and finish it on the back. And it could give the shirts away. However, most church members would be willing to buy such a T-shirt if it promoted their church or propagated the mission.

7. BROCHURE

Over the past few years a number of parachurch ministries, such as private schools, have seen the value of producing informational brochures. This is because so many don't have the same exposure to the Christian and non-Christian public as the institutional church. In some cases, they have to do this to survive.

Some churches have adopted the use of the brochure to advertise their ministries. This is becoming increasingly important in the information age in which people want to know something about a ministry before they will frequent it. Brochure contents provide a wide range of information such as the name, location, phone number, times of services, various programs, a brief doctrinal statement, a denominational affiliation, and a simple map. Many identify their senior pastor and include a picture. Their purpose is to attract visitors and apprise potential members of what the church is all about.

▼▼▼

The informational brochure, when nicely done, provides an excellent medium through which a ministry can propagate its mission.

▲▲▲

Though not enough ministries use it this way, the informational brochure, when nicely done, provides an excellent medium through which a ministry can propagate its mission. While the more established Christian institutions aren't using it for this purpose, a number of newer and recently planted ministries have begun to include their consensual mission statement as well as their core values and vision in the brochure.

8. PERFORMANCE APPRAISAL

There is an old saying: What gets evaluated gets done. A growing number of companies use their core mission as a key determiner in evaluating the performance of their employees, including managers. The company also recruits its people using the mission as a primary vehicle. They tell potential employees: "This is what we're all about. This is what we're attempting to accomplish. Do you want to be a part of doing this? We will use this to evaluate your performance."

In many ways this is fair and seems like a great idea. Everyone is expected to know the mission statement, and, therefore, exactly what the company expects from them. They become a part of the company based on their desire to help the business accomplish its mission. In the process, everybody knows well the corporate mission, and they are judged by how well they follow it, contribute to it, and help realize it.

While this makes sense in the marketplace, some believe that this might be too harsh for the church or parachurch. I disagree. Why can't Christian organizations clearly explain their mission to their people, and then evaluate their performance accordingly? The problem with far too many ministries, especially the church, is that they have a staff of people who either don't know the mission or aren't on board with the mission. Acceptance of Christ's mission must be a requirement for acceptance into the church. This sends a clear message of the importance of the mission to the ministry from the very beginning. And the mission is propagated even further when the church uses it to evaluate the performance of its staff and volunteers. Again, what gets evaluated, gets done.

Some would object to using the mission statement to recruit and evaluate volunteers. This is because volunteers are in high demand but in such short supply. However, I would argue that it's better not to have a volunteer than to have one who disagrees with your core institutional mission. A difference over mission would also indicate that the volunteer differs with the core values that drive the ministry. Over time, such volunteers place the ministry in jeopardy.

9. BULLETIN OR NEWSLETTER

A wise ministry knows the importance of communicating with its people. This takes place most often through a letter, bulletin, or newsletter. Most Christian organizations have been doing this for years. The average congregant has grown used to receiving information about the church or parachurch ministry through the mail. When people walk into church, they expect to receive a bulletin that communicates any announcements and the order of the service. In fact, some become upset when the church runs out of bulletins or fails to provide one for them.

▼▼▼

The bulletin or newsletter is an important vehicle to propagate the ministry's mission.

▲▲▲

The bulletin or newsletter is an important vehicle to propagate the ministry's mission. Your ministry could place the mission statement in a conspicuous place in the newsletter so that it receives maximum attention every time it's distributed. Figure 6.2 presents the bulletin of my church, Northwood Community Church in Dallas, Texas. We have placed our mission statement in a prominent location below our logo. However, the problem with including it every time is that after a while, people begin to ignore it. Come up with creative ways to display your mission in these vehicles. You could place it in different places on the page or move it around from page to page. One time you might want to feature it, another time you could simply include it.

Northwood
Community Church
Developing people into fully functioning followers of Christ

Figure 6.2

These nine suggestions should get the ideas flowing. I recommend using two or more in combination. Other ideas like placing the mission statement on such things as billboards, marquees, coffee mugs, ball-point pens, pins, or buttons may be used. Be aware, however, that some may find these practices, or any of the nine, objectionable. Some people feel these items create a carnival-like atmosphere in God's house. Ministry leaders should use discretion so as not to offend the people they are trying to reach.

QUESTIONS FOR THOUGHT AND DISCUSSION

1. What is the difference between casting a vision and propagating a mission?

2. Does your life model your ministry's mission? Do other leaders in your ministry, both staff and laypeople, model the mission?

3. Are you willing to put the statement on a wall plaque? Where would you place it to get the most attention?

4. Would placing your mission on wallet-size cards aid in propagating that mission? Would the production of a mission video aid in propagating your mission? Would your people accept or reject these methods?

5. Does your ministry conduct some kind of class for new people such as a new members' or newcomers' class? If yes, does the ministry use this class as an opportunity to convey its mission? Why or why not?

6. Has your ministry produced a brochure? If yes, does it convey the ministry's mission? Is your bulletin or newsletter a good place to propagate your mission?

7. Does your ministry ever evaluate its personnel? If yes, is the mission used as an important part of that evaluation? Why or why not?

8. Would your people wear a T-shirt with the statement on the front or back?

9. How do you respond to the idea of using some other method for propagating the mission such as a billboard, marquee, coffee mug, ball-point pen, or a button pinned on a lapel or coat

pocket? How would your members and target group respond? Will you attempt any of these?

10. What are some other ways to propagate your mission that aren't mentioned in this chapter?

ENDNOTES

1. Peter F. Drucker, *Managing for the Future: The 1990s and Beyond,* (New York: Truman Talley Books, 1992), 219.

2. See Aubrey Malphurs, *Developing a Vision for Ministry in the 21st Century* (Grand Rapids: Baker Book House, 1992), chap. 5.

3. Patricia Jones and Larry Kahaner, *Say It & Live It* (New York: Doubleday, 1995), 266.

7

The Implementation of the Mission
Your Strategy—The Key to Implementing Your Mission

There was a new spirit that pervaded Grace Community Church. It seemed as though God was moving in a fresh way to revitalize the ministry. Everyone sensed it and wanted to be a part of it. The church was gaining a sense of significance that it had not known in a long time. The consensual, dynamic mission gave the church direction. Over the years, the founding mission had been neglected and lost, leaving the church to wander from Christ's intent. The mission was back, and the congregation now understood what they were supposed to be doing.

One of the reasons for the excitement was the clear propagation of the mission. The statement was framed and hung in a prominent place in the church's foyer as well as on Pastor Larry's wall. The ushers passed out wallet-size cards to be kept in accessible places like wallets and purses. One Sunday, Pastor Larry took off his jacket to reveal a T-shirt with the mission statement on the front and back. He announced that the church would supply anyone with a free T-shirt if they'd simply agree to wear it. Those who attended the new members' class gave the instructor high marks for his creativity in conveying the church's mission.

In spite of all this activity, Pastor Larry Brown knew that the biggest challenge lay ahead. Their mission statement answered the first question: What are we supposed to be doing? Implementing a strategy, however, would mean much change for his people. They had been good about accepting ownership of the mission, but would they respond as well to major changes in the church's culture?

The essence of Grace Community Church's mission and the Savior's command is to make disciples. This chapter will help you understand and think through a disciple-making process that will enable your ministry to implement its mission. I have divided it into two sections. The first will coach you on the preparation necessary for developing your strategy. The second will walk you through the process of strategy development.[1]

THE PREPARATION FOR DEVELOPING YOUR STRATEGY

Before you begin to craft a strategy that is unique to your church, some initial preparation is essential. This preparation lays a broad, general foundation on which the strategy development process will build. Three areas for preparation include the need for, importance of, and definition of a strategy.

The Need for a Strategy

Bob Gilliam of the Evangelical Free Church developed the Spiritual Journey Evaluation. He used it to survey almost four thousand attendees in thirty-five churches in several denominations from Florida to Washington. He discovered that most people in these churches are not growing spiritually. Of those taking the survey, 24 percent indicated that their behavior was sliding backwards and 41 percent said they were "static" in their spiritual growth. Thus, 65 percent are either arrested or in decline in their growth toward Christlikeness. The verdict is in. Very few churches in North America are making disciples.

▼▼▼

Few churches have a strategy for making disciples.

▲▲▲

Why aren't churches making disciples? It is because few churches have a strategy for making disciples. Most realize its importance but are depending on a more "caught than taught" strategy or what I call "discipleship by osmosis." They hope in vain that somehow people will do it on their own. The problem is that most people won't. And if they aren't discipled soon after coming to faith, the chances are overwhelming that they will slip into nominal Christianity and likely join the ranks of the unchurched. They become like the seed in the Parable of the Sower that fell on rocky places and fell away when trouble and persecution came (Matt. 13:20–21). Or they are like the seed that fell among the thorns and were choked by the worries of this life and the deceitfulness of wealth (Matt. 13:22).

The Importance of Strategy

A compelling strategy is vital to your ministry for three prominent reasons.

▼▼▼

*A dynamic strategy accomplishes
your ministry mission.*

▲▲▲

A dynamic strategy accomplishes your ministry mission. While you may have the most profound mission the world has ever witnessed, without a strategy—a way to implement that mission—then you are wasting your time and that of others who emotionally and intellectually own your mission. It is your strategy that moves people from where they are spiritually (lost or immature) to where God wants them to be (Christlike or mature). Most Christians simply don't know how to become a disciple. That is where the strategy fits in. A good one aids your people in accomplishing the biblical goal that is central and vital to their lives and your ministry.

▼▼▼

A good strategy facilitates understanding.

▲▲▲

A good strategy facilitates understanding. One thing that most churches have in common is their programs. Over the years most churches have, with little thought, added many programs, one on top of the other like layers of paint. The problem is that people (and I suspect the pastors) don't understand how these programs work together to make disciples. The result is that most of them don't, and some even work against one another.

It is at the strategy level that the various programs work together to produce godly disciples. A well-developed strategy ties all the programs together and communicates the spiritual purposes of each. First comes the strategy; then programs are developed around that strategy. Each program is designed to accomplish some phase of the strategy. When a program ceases to accomplish anything, it must be replaced by one that does.

Regardless, the strategy communicates to your people what they have to do to become Christ's disciples and precisely where they are in that process. The people of Willow Creek Community Church in

Barrington, Illinois, understand that their weekend services target unbelievers exclusively and their midweek services are for believers. Consequently, they bring their lost friends to church on weekends, and they look to the midweek services for their own spiritual growth.

The third reason the strategy is important is that it supplies a sense of momentum and progress. People can sense when a church isn't doing much for them spiritually—when not much is happening. The response of the preboomer generation was to patiently stay with the church. The response of the boomer generation and Generation X is to find another church or drop out all together.

The solution, however, is for the church to implement a high impact, disciple-making strategy and communicate it clearly to their people. To accomplish this, some churches have adopted the illustration of a baseball diamond (figure 7.1). Each base represents a step in the disciple-making process. At first base, you become a disciple. At second base, you become a growing disciple. At third, you become a serving disciple, and when you reach home plate, you become a disciple maker. People know what base they're on, and thus understand where they are at any moment in the process. They can look back and see how far they have come and be encouraged. They can also look ahead and be challenged. As they gradually move around the base paths, they feel a sense of momentum. They realize that as they work their way through the various programs, they're making progress.

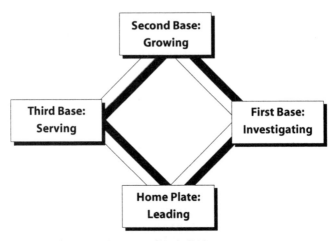

Figure 7.1: Baseball Diagram

The Definition of a Strategy

Now that you understand the need for and the importance of a dynamic strategy, I'll provide a definition for the term as I'm using it in this chapter. I define a strategy as the process that determines how you will accomplish the mission of your ministry. This definition has three important concepts.

A strategy has a mission. Every ministry must have a mission. Without the mission or ministry end, it will go nowhere. That's the whole point of this book. My experience in working with churches, however, is that few have clear, succinct missions. Again, the mission asks the important question: What are we supposed to be doing? The answer for the church is found in the Savior's words in Matthew 28:19–20 where he commands us to go into all the world and make disciples. Every church must ask the first question and then ask: What are we really doing? This is the mission audit of chapter 4. If a discrepancy exists between the two, then the church will need to make the necessary changes to bring itself in line with what the Savior wants it to do.

A strategy involves a process. A good strategy includes a process. According to Scripture it's the process of moving people from prebirth to maturity (Matt. 28:19–20; Col. 1:28; 2:6–7). This involves accepting people where they are in relation to Christ (lost or saved) and moving them to where God wants them to be (saved and mature). Every person is responsible to accept Christ, and each Christian is responsible to grow in Christ. In Colossians 2:6–7, Paul writes: "So then, just as you received Christ Jesus as Lord, continue to live in him, rooted and built up in him, strengthened in the faith as you were taught, and overflowing with thankfulness." And it's the church's responsibility to help Christians move toward maturity. Again, Paul writes in Colossians 1:28: "We proclaim him, admonishing and teaching everyone with all wisdom, so that we may present everyone perfect in Christ." This involves providing a disciple-making process to help believers accomplish their spiritual objectives. Therefore, to serve your people, your church must have a strategy in place that potentially moves all of them to Christlikeness.

A strategy answers the question: How? Finally, a good strategy addresses another key question: How will you achieve your mission? What means will you use? The ministry means enable you to accomplish the ministry end. For example, your mission may be to climb Mount Everest. The strategy determines how you'll get from where you are—the bottom of the mountain—to the top. Specifically, the strategy is the action steps that you take to get there. You must realize that your ministry has a strategy. The question is, Is it a good one? A good strategy is one that is fulfilling the ministry's mission.

THE PROCESS FOR DEVELOPING YOUR STRATEGY

Now that you have a foundation for the development of a disciple-making strategy, you can begin to build upon that foundation. The strategy development process is fourfold, and like the mission development process consists of four *p*s: the preparation, the person, the program, and the plan.

The Preparation for the Strategy

In this section, we move into the actual "hands on" preparation necessary to begin the strategy development process. You'll see that the process here is similar to the one for developing your mission in chapter 4. Let this serve as a quick review of that process but note that a few differences exist. The preparation for strategy development consists of six elements.

Need. The question here is whether or not the ministry is ready to begin the process. The ministry leaders may not be convinced that a real need exists for a new or different strategy. When this is the case, they will drag their feet and not much happens. The solution to this problem is to conduct a number of audits, the most important of which is the general audit. It encourages the leadership to identify the ministry's strengths, limitations, and weaknesses. If this doesn't surface the need, then the leaders can perform additional ministry audits such as a performance audit (how are we doing?), a mission audit (are we accomplishing the church's mission?) as well as others.[2]

▼▼▼

*Simply because leaders recognize
the need for a strategy, doesn't mean that
the ministry is ready to develop one.*

▲▲▲

Readiness. Assuming the need, the next question is, Is the organization ready for a strategy? Simply because leaders recognize the need for a strategy, doesn't mean that the ministry is ready to develop one. One criterion is their openness to change. The ministry's willingness to make some, if not all, the needed changes reflects its change readiness. Another criterion of readiness is the attitude of the primary ministry leader. The strategy needs the support of this person in particular in order to be carried out. A third criterion is the attitude of the ministry board. If the leadership board wants to develop a powerful strategy, the chances that it will happen are even greater.

Personnel. When a ministry decides to craft a strategy, it must determine who will accomplish the project. As with the mission statement, this is the primary responsibility of the leadership, and the point leader of the team in particular, such as the pastor of a church. This person is responsible for the initial development; however, he or she is not to attempt the entire process alone. Having completed the initial draft, the point person must allow others to get their "fingerprints" all over the process as well. If this doesn't happen, then other leaders and ministry personnel will not take ownership of the new strategy nor be an effective part of its implementation.

Time. Since few people have much discretionary time, how much time it will take to craft a disciple-making strategy is a key question. Much depends on the criteria above; if the leader of the ministry or the board is behind the move, the process will go faster. I would predict that on average it will take much longer to develop strategy than to draft a mission, ranging from ten to twenty full days. Most would accomplish this in a number of meetings lasting several hours. One caution: It usually takes longer than you think.

Cost. How much it will cost to develop a high impact strategy is situational and depends on such items as salaries, food and lodging, demographic and psychographic materials, and the use of consultants. While it will likely cost more than the development of a mission, most of these expenses, if incurred, can be kept to a minimum. However, use of such factors as a consultant will result in a better product.

Place. The strategy planning team will need a space where they can operate. Many use their own facilities. When it's possible, however, using a retreat or some place that is geographically removed from the normal work area is preferable. Foremost, it eliminates distractions. Even the Savior chose to retreat to a solitary place for times of prayer (Mark 1:35). Regardless of where the team goes to craft the strategy, it must provide them with maximum opportunity to work creatively and efficiently.

The Person of the Strategy

Once people are prepared to develop a strategy, the next step is to discover the ministry's target group. One reason why so many North American churches are struggling and dying is that they are attempting to reach everyone in general with the result that they reach no one in particular. It is theologically sound to reach as many people as possible. The church must be ready to present the gospel to anyone, anywhere, at any time. Otherwise, it leans in the direction of discrimination.

▼▼▼

Once people are prepared to develop a strategy, the next step is to discover the ministry's target group.

▲▲▲

Reality, however, is that people don't respond to just any church. Right or wrong, they are attracted to churches that address their needs and where people are like them. Regardless, the church has two audiences. The first is their own people who have in some way identified with the church (the constituency or churched). The second is those who are outside the church (both lost and saved). Most have focused on the former and ignored the latter. The parachurch organization has a more focused audience. In most cases, a parachurch ministry exists to reach a particular target group such as children, college students, international students, and others. Consequently, much of the following is addressed to churches.

As a part of its strategy, the church needs to target those outside its four walls as well as those within. The following four steps should prove helpful.

Identify your target group. This involves several theological and philosophical questions. Will you target lost or saved people? Teaching churches mostly target the saved, and evangelistic churches mostly target the lost. Don't we need to target both? While 80 percent of churches are targeting the churched, approximately 80 percent of North Americans are unchurched. Will you in some way target seekers? They are lost people who, through the convicting work of the Holy Spirit (John 16:7–11), are interested in spiritual truth.

And keep in mind there are many groups of people who might ask, Will you target people "like us"? Right or wrong, most people respond best to churches that reflect their culture. While Paul, who was gifted cross-culturally (Eph. 3:7–8), chose to minister cross-culturally to the Gentiles, Peter chose to minister inter-culturally to the Jews (Gal. 2:7).

Finally, will you target needy people? One way that God has chosen to get the attention of lost people and to minister to them is through their perceived or felt needs. As you minister to their felt needs, you gain the right to minister to their real needs—their spiritual needs. Consequently, Christ fed the multitudes physically as he fed them spiritually (John 6:1–15).

Locate your target geographically. There are five questions that function as a funnel in helping you to locate your target group. Where in the world is your target group? Where in the country? Where in the state or province? Where in a city or town? And where in your immediate community? The first question is broad like the top of a funnel, and the last is small and focused like the bottom or end of the funnel.

Gather information about your target. This primarily involves two kinds of information. One is demographics, which provide such information as age, sex, occupation, income, race, marital status, and other data. The other is psychographics, which provide such information as people's needs, hopes, dreams, aspirations, and so on. Some other sources that could be helpful are dominant trends and any current historical events that might affect the target group.

Construct a profile person. This involves collecting and synthesizing all the information gathered from steps 1 through 3. You should take this information and use it to construct a profile person who summarizes all the characteristics of your target person. This serves to emphasize outreach and to remind your people of whom you're trying to reach. You might depict the profile person as a cartoon-type character and dress him or her in clothing, formal or casual, that characterizes your target. If your target people are highly interested in tennis, then dress them in tennis clothing and put rackets in their hands.

The Program of the Strategy

Once you've identified your target group, you're ready to take the third step in the process of developing your strategy. Here you must ask: What kind of church will it take to minister to the people outside our four walls as well as inside them? This is a critical strategy question, and there are a number of questions you may ask to help you in formulating your answer.

▼▼▼

What kind of church will it take to minister to the people outside our four walls as well as inside them?

▲▲▲

What kinds of ministries are reaching people around the world and in North America? You would be wise to examine what church and parachurch ministries are doing, internationally and nationally, that God is blessing. There are a number of exemplary churches and parachurch ministries around the world that can give you significant ideas for your strategy. However, you should also give special attention to those that are ministering in spiritual and sociological contexts similar to your own. You would also benefit by keeping your finger on the pulse of those ministries that are struggling. Taking note of a variety of other ministries helps you learn much about what to do and what not to do.

What kinds of ministries are reaching people in your ministry area? It's imperative that you explore ministries "close to home" because they will teach what may or may not work in your unique ministry context. You need to identify the church and parachurch ministries in your community that God is blessing. You will learn from them so that you may benefit from their wise choices while not repeating their mistakes. As above, include the struggling churches in your study.

What kind of church will it take to reach your target group? Working through the Strategy Program Worksheet will help you determine the methods or functions you'll need to minister to your people and target group.

Strategy Program Worksheet

Decisions must be made about specific methods or functions needed to reach your target. Decision one concerns the kinds of meetings necessary to minister to people. The best kinds of meetings are those that accomplish your purposes. As to size, there are three options. You may choose one or a combination of the following:

- Large group meetings
- Medium size meetings
- Small group meetings

Decision two is worship style. What kind of worship will characterize your ministry?

- A traditional style
- A contemporary style
- A combination

Decision three is community: How will people relate to one another? Relating involves living and experiencing the "one another" passages of the Scriptures. There are many choices. Here are a few:

- Safely
- Authentically
- Lovingly
- Encouragingly
- Truthfully

Decision four is teaching. Good expository teaching is vital to any ministry, especially the church. One issue involves the people who do the teaching.

- The professional staff and a handful of lay people as the primary teachers
- The gifted lay people as well as the professionals as the primary teachers

Decision five is evangelism. The issue here isn't whether the church does evangelism. That is assumed. The issue is over who does most of the evangelism.

- The professionals do the evangelism (pastors, missionaries, traveling evangelists).
- The people do most of the evangelism.

Decision six is missions. Again, the issue isn't over the inclusion of missions in the program. The issue is the geographical focus of missions.

- We will promote foreign missions (finances and prayer).
- We will promote both foreign and home missions (finances, prayer, and short term missions trips).[3]

Decision seven is leadership. Every organization must have good leadership. The question is who leads.

- The role of the professional person is to lead.
- The role of lay people, as well as the professional, is to lead.

Decision eight is preaching. One issue is the kind of sermons, and the other is the kind of preacher.

- The kind of sermons
  Longer (45–50 minutes)
  Shorter (20–40 minutes)

Evangelistic
Expository

- The kind of preacher
  Only the pastor
  A team: the pastor and associates
  Gifted lay people
  A combination

Decision nine is communication. Every ministry must have an accurate communication system both within and without the church.

- Communication within the ministry
  Announcements
  Bulletin
  Newsletter
  Slide-tape presentation
  E-mail
  Snap mail
  Post-its
  Memos
  Word of mouth

- Communication outside the ministry
  Word of mouth
  Advertising
  Direct mail
  Telemarketing
  America Online

Decision ten is giving. Unfortunately every ministry, no matter how spiritual, needs funding to operate its ministries. The issue is how to approach people for money.

- Take an offering during the service
- Messages from the pulpit on giving
- Fund drives
- A biblical stewardship program
- Take an offering in the small group meetings

Decision eleven is care. Churches are responsible to take care of their people. The question is: Who does the caring?

- The pastor
- A minister of pastoral care
- A lay pastor
- A lay small-group leader
- The members of a small group

Decision twelve is Christian education. How will people learn about the Scriptures, theology, and the Christian faith?

- A Sunday school program
- Small group ministries
- Staff and lay-led seminars

Decision thirteen is ministry. Specifically, who does the work of the ministry?

- The pastor
- The pastoral staff
- Gifted lay people
- A combination of the above

Decision fourteen is special services. Often, these are services above and beyond those provided by most ministries.

- Food and clothing
- Shelter
- Street mission
- Medical and psychological help
- Divorce recovery
- 10K run, health fair, crime watch, and others

Decision fifteen is facilities. While appearance is important, the facility must also be functional.

- New or older facility
- Church or nonchurch architecture
- Well equipped
- Clean

Decision sixteen is the name of the ministry. Some might innocently ask: What's in a name? The answer is everything, because the name serves to attract or repel. People determine attendance or nonattendance based on the name of the organization.

- Denominational name
- Nondenominational name

Decision seventeen is the atmosphere or mood of worship. How should people feel and look in the church's services?

- Quiet and reverent
- Excited and expectant
- Formal attire
- Casual attire

Once you and your ministry have thought through these decisions, the programs that appear as an important part of your strategy will be much clearer.

The Plan of the Strategy

A strategy doesn't exist by itself. Other vital elements are necessary to craft a significant strategy that will both minister to your people and reach out to those in your community. These elements are an important part of the larger strategic plan to implement your programs. Scripture contains a number of passages that encourage believers to plan (Luke 14:28–30; Prov. 15:22; 16:3–4). The simple principle is that what gets planned most likely will get done.

▼▼▼

What gets planned most likely will get done.

▲▲▲

The ministry plan serves as a blueprint that dictates all the decisions a leader will make as he or she implements the strategy. A good plan consists of a statement of need, core values, a mission, a vision, the strategy, resources (personnel and budget), a schedule, and regular evaluation.[4]

A statement of need. A planning document opens with a statement that addresses why the community needs your ministry. It answers the question: Why is this ministry in this community? The information in the need statement comes from any audits and the demographic and psychographic studies you've conducted on your ministry area. The purpose behind the need statement is to present a problem or challenge that the rest of the plan solves or meets.

The core values. The first step toward resolving the need expressed in the above statement is the ministry's credo or statement of core organizational values. Every ministry has certain basic, core values, good and bad, that drive it. The significance of these values is that they control all behavior and influence every decision that leaders make. You would be wise to know your ministry's core values as well as your own and place the former in a ministry credo that's regularly communicated to your people and the ministry community. This alerts all to the hidden motivators that explain why you do what you do.

The mission. The next element in the planning document, and a vital part of the same, is the ministry's mission statement. It should follow the values because they dictate the precise mission you select. The mission statement, as we've learned in this book, serves to provide the direction and clarify the function of the ministry. While Christ has predetermined the church's mission statement as the Great Commission, you will need to craft it so that your people can understand it.

The vision. After the mission statement comes the vision. Because it's a "seeing" concept and functions best in a verbal not a visual context, its use in a plan is limited and optional. Unlike the mission statement, you may or may not want to place it in your planning document. If you choose to include it, then it should be longer than the mission statement but less than a page or people may quickly tire of it. The advantage of including it is that it will provide a snapshot of what the mission will look like as it's being realized in your ministry community.

The strategy. The mission statement affects not only the ministry's vision but its strategy. The vision is what the ministry will look like as it accomplishes the mission in its unique community. As stated earlier in this chapter, the strategy is the vehicle for accomplishing the mission. It answers the important question: How will we accomplish the mission? Like the mission statement, the strategy statement is and must be a vital part of the planning document.

The resources. The resources for your ministry are twofold: Your personnel and budget. Your ministry will only be as good as the people who staff it. A good ministry is staffed with happy, productive people; a poor or struggling ministry most often is staffed with unhappy, unproductive people. A criterion for good staffing is that people minister in their areas of expertise. And the key to implementing this criterion is helping people discover how God has designed them (their divine design) and placing them in positions that honor their design.

A fact of leadership is that it takes finances to operate a ministry— even the most lean ones. Every ministry will incur expenses in its daily operation, and the leadership is responsible to secure sufficient funding to meet these expenses. Remember: What gets funded, often gets done.

The schedule. A plan needs a schedule. The reason is that it determines when you do what you do. A simple fact is that if something doesn't get scheduled, it doesn't get done. Consequently, whatever you deem as important to your ministry must be scheduled.

The evaluation. Another fact of ministry life is that what gets evaluated gets done. However, far too many ministries in general, and churches in particular, fail to evaluate what they're doing. Regular evaluation is essential to a ministry if it's to improve and better serve its constituency. Proverbs 15:22 says: "Plans fail for lack of counsel, but with many advisers they succeed." A key evaluative question is, How can we do it better next time? Everyone in your ministry should be encouraged to ask this question at least monthly if not weekly. In addition, this approach to ministry improvement allows for change from the grassroots up.

QUESTIONS FOR THOUGHT AND DISCUSSION

1. Name several ministries like yours that God is blessing overseas and in North America. What are they doing that others aren't? What can you learn from them that might be helpful in your ministry?

2. Name some ministries like yours that God is blessing in your community. What are they doing that the struggling ministries like them aren't? What can you learn about ministry from them?

3. Name some of the ministries like yours in your community that are struggling. What are they doing? What can they teach you about what not to do?

4. Which of the three generational groups (preboomer, boomer, Generation X) are present in your church? How will their presence affect the programs that make up your strategy? How will you minister to the people inside the church and outside the church at the same time?

5. Of the seventeen decisions regarding your selection of programs for your strategy, which were the easiest to answer? Why? Which were the most difficult to answer? Why? Which of your answers surprised you the most? Why?

6. Do you have a ministry plan? Why or why not? Does your ministry plan include a statement of need, your core values, mission, vision, strategy, resources, schedule, and evaluation? If not all, then which ones?

ENDNOTES

1. See Aubrey Malphurs, *Strategy 2000* (Grand Rapids: Kregel Publications, 1996).
2. Ibid., chap. 5 for more information about these various ministry audits.
3. I believe that just as some of the old paradigm churches overreacted toward foreign missions and virtually ignored home missions, so the new paradigm churches are ignoring foreign missions in favor of home missions. Neither extreme is healthy for world evangelization.
4. For examples of each of the following, see Malphurs, *Strategy 2000* (Grand Rapids: Kregel Publications, 1996), chap. 8.

8

The Preservation of the Mission
Nine Ways to Preserve Your Mission

Surprisingly, the ministry at Grace Community Church continues to go well for Pastor Larry Brown. I use the term *surprisingly* because revitalizing established churches isn't easy. Most churches, whether planted or revitalized, pass through a period of ministry turbulence. Just as most airplanes encounter weather turbulence somewhere between takeoff and landing, so ministries periodically pass through times of turbulence. Some problematic churches seem to remain in a season of turbulence. When a ministry flies through turbulent times, the leaders in general and the pastor in particular must tightly fasten their seat belts and stay on course, or risk straying from the flight plan and missing their destination.

Grace Community Church has crafted and implemented a new disciple-making strategy that the majority of the church has accepted with unabated enthusiasm. Pastor Larry has challenged his people to make a difference in the community. He's challenged them to Christlikeness. In doing so, he's discovered that a significant number of his people hunger and thirst for righteousness (Matt. 5:6). Revival is taking place in the midst of the ministry. Many of his people want to know how to "grow in the grace and knowledge of our Lord and Savior Jesus Christ" (2 Peter 3:18).

However, Pastor Larry must anticipate ministry turbulence. It happens to the best of churches. And it's during these times that the ministry and the mission become most vulnerable. Opposition ignites ministry fires and the leadership becomes so busy fighting the fires that they lose sight of the church's mission. Somehow it becomes lost in the shuffle of problem solving. Regardless, when you lose sight of the mission you are lost. Consequently, every leader must work hard at the preservation of the mission. But what is involved in mission preservation? How do leaders keep their ministries from losing their mission and thus their direction and function? Before answering these questions, we must first probe the problems that may lead to the erosion of a ministry's mission. In this section, I'll focus on three: conflict, compromise, and success.

CONFLICT

Every ministry whether large or small, growing or declining, new paradigm or old paradigm will experience interpersonal conflict. It happened to the early church in the Book of Acts. Luke notes in Acts 4:32 that in the Jerusalem church, "All the believers were one in heart and mind." This is the ideal that all ministries aim for and some such as the Jerusalem church realized. But not for long. Ananias, probably a member of the church, sold some property and gave the money to the ministry (Acts 5:1–2). Actually, he held back some of the money while giving the impression that he had given it all. God dealt strongly with Ananias and resolved the conflict (Acts 5:3–5).

Another conflict, possibly of racial origin, is recorded in Acts 6:1–7. Those who were responsible for the daily distribution of food to the church's widows (probably the Hebraic Jews) overlooked the Grecian Jewish widows (Acts 6:1). In this situation, the leadership acted quickly to resolve the problem by assigning the responsibility for this "soup kitchen" ministry to other qualified leaders (Acts 6:2–6).

▼▼▼

If conflict happened in the first century church,
then it will happen in the twenty-first century church.

▲▲▲

If conflict happened in the first century church, then it will happen in the twenty-first century church. I'm unaware of any ministry that hasn't experienced some kind of conflict. I don't believe that such a work exists. Consequently, Pastor Larry Brown must be ready to deal with any conflict if he's not to become sidetracked and lose sight of the ministry's mission.

COMPROMISE

In the two conflict situations in Acts 5 and 6, the church faced and dealt with the problems quickly and without compromise. To its disadvantage, today's average church fails to handle conflict that way. The typical lay board consciously or unconsciously believes their job is to keep the peace. When a problem arises, they do everything possible to make everyone happy in hopes that the problem will go away. Most often this takes the form of compromise. Though compromise seems fair—everyone has to give a little—no one is completely happy with the results and the ministry suffers. Just as important, how can you compromise the church's mission? Since that mission is the Great Commission, how can you compromise that without causing irreparable damage?

▼▼▼

The solution to ministry conflict is consensus, not compromise.

▲▲▲

The solution to ministry conflict is consensus, not compromise. This is how the early church dealt with conflict as illustrated at the Jerusalem Council in Acts 15. Those who lead ministries and make up ministry boards must agree to disagree. What this means is that everyone should be heard on a particular issue where there is disagreement (vv. 5–12). However, when the group makes a decision, those who disagree need to support that decision as best they can, despite feelings to the contrary. The possible exception is on major doctrinal issues. The worst response is to verbally attack the final decision among the ministry's constituency. This leads only to strife and schism and the potential demise of the organization.

SUCCESS

Every ministry, like every person, experiences a life cycle (figure 8.1). This is because the ministry consists of people. A ministry such as a church is born and experiences a period of sustained growth. At some point, however, it plateaus. If it fails to get off that plateau and resume normal healthy growth, it will decline. At the beginning of the third millennium, 80 to 85 percent of the churches in North America are in serious decline.

When should a church deal with a ministry decline? The answer is, Before you get there. The time to deal with ministry decline is during times of ministry success. By success, I mean that you are accomplishing your mission, such as making disciples. Success isn't a good teacher. It can seduce even the best leaders and their constituency into thinking that they can't fail. Most hazardous, success has a way of lulling them to sleep. All of a sudden they awaken to find the ministry in a downward spiral.

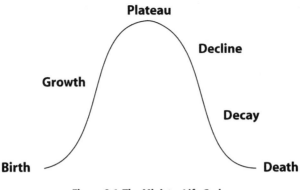

Figure 8.1: The Ministry Life Cycle

Successful ministries become prone to inward-looking. Because they're successful, people assume that they're doing all the right things so they commit to institutionalizing what they're doing. Rather than evaluating what they are supposed to be doing, they institutionalize what they're doing. They become brittle and inflexible. Over time this serves only to inhibit the ministry and send it into a severe decline.

▼▼▼

The time to deal with ministry decline is during times of ministry success.

▲▲▲

As I study churches that stay at the top, I note that they don't allow success to lull them to sleep or make them brittle and inflexible. They regularly take the pulse of their people and their ministry community and adjust what they're doing to be even more effective at realizing their mission. For example, Willow Creek Community Church outside of Chicago, Illinois, has been very successful at targeting and reaching baby boomers. However, recently they added to their pastoral staff a man who has been very good at reaching the next generation—Generation X.

▼▼▼

Churches that stay at the top, don't allow success to lull them to sleep.

▲▲▲

What about a church that's already in decline? It's not impossible to revitalize a declining ministry such as Grace Community Church. A growing number of churches sprinkled all across North America have demonstrated this. However, the proverbial "an ounce of prevention is worth a pound of cure" is always the better prescription.

Now that we have looked at three critical problems that lead to the demise of a ministry's mission, it's time to see what's involved in mission preservation. How do leaders keep their ministry ships from losing or forgetting their destinations and thus drifting off course? The following practices will aid in mission preservation.

1. PROPAGATING

Your ministry can develop and own an excellent mission that is authentic and biblical in every way. However, if the ministry fails to propagate that mission, then it is destined to drift away from it. Mission propagation was the topic in chapter 6. What is important to understand in this chapter is that the propagation of the mission also serves to preserve the mission. The two work hand in glove.

In chapter 6, I presented nine ways that a ministry can propagate its mission. The most important is the leader's life. A leader who incarnates the mission also preserves the mission. The life of a leader is under constant scrutiny. Followers regularly ask: Does this person live what he or she says? When the answer is yes, it serves not only to communicate the mission, but the leader's physical presence regularly reminds them of it. They can't get it out of their heads and the mission is preserved.

▼▼▼

A leader who incarnates the mission
also preserves the mission.

▲▲▲

A wall plaque, wallet-size cards, a video presentation, classes, or a newsletter also serve to propagate the mission. The power of these methods is that they keep the mission before the people. They give the ministry mission physical presence. Objects such as T-shirts, a banner, or a brochure attract people's attention and jog their memories. Regular exposure leads to implementation and preservation.

2. RECRUITING

Another method for preserving the mission is recruiting. Recruitment is attraction. Not only does a biblical mission statement serve to keep the people in the ministry on course, but it attracts people outside the ministry who share the same mission. When you recruit people with the same mission, you take a giant step in mission preservation. This includes not only members as with a church, but professional staff and lay leadership. You must always look for absolute agreement on the mission before considering a new staff person or moving lay people into key leadership positions within the ministry. To do otherwise is to court disaster.

▼▼▼

When you recruit people with the same mission,
you take a giant step in mission preservation.

▲▲▲

If over time your ministry attracts people who have their own mission, then you put the preservation of your mission in jeopardy. Should you attract a number of these people, it's only a matter of time before they outnumber those who own your mission, and the ministry shifts to another mission, or to no mission, and is set adrift. However, those who hold to a different mission don't have to be in the majority to send a church into decline. A vocal minority can accomplish the same. Unfortunately, a vocal minority is heard far above the sounds made by a quiet majority.

3. ENFOLDING

Once people are recruited to the ministry, the next step is to enfold them into it. In the church, enfolding is the process of membership. In a parachurch ministry, it is hiring or accepting volunteers for service. Recruiting brings people up close to but still outside that ministry. Enfolding moves them from outside the ministry into the ministry.

Most churches require that people who desire to be a part of the ministry join the ministry. This is an excellent way to protect and preserve the mission. A requirement for membership or employment is agreement with the church's dynamic core mission as well as its core values. One wonders why people would want to join or work for any organization that is moving in a direction that is different from their own destination? Perhaps the answer is a friendship or an attraction to a church's worship format or an opportunity to get some ministry experience. Regardless, over time friendships wane, worship formats change, and experience is gained. All that may be left is a strong aversion to the church's desired direction.

4. INCULTURATING

It's not enough to recruit and enfold. Once people join a ministry, they can change their minds. Some may also forget or lose their enthusiasm for the mission. Others may have nodded their heads in assent while not really understanding the mission. And then some will always "slip through the cracks." Inculturating instills and reinforces the mission among those who are a part of the ministry.

▼▼▼

Inculturating instills and reinforces the mission among those who are a part of the ministry.

▲▲▲

The bulletin, a newsletter, the T-shirt, and similar propagation tools from chapter 6 aid in this process. However, there are other methods. The leader or someone on the leadership team might write a letter periodically to the constituency. Some leaders could visit small-group ministries and discuss and answer questions on the mission. Personal visitation underlines for people the importance of the topic. The ministry staff could make heroes of those who in some way promote the mission. Reference to the mission could be the standard first step in resolving conflicts.

5. TRAINING

A legitimate, biblical expectation is that all who become a part of a ministry will in some way serve that ministry. However, in the church some people hide behind a pew where they simply "sit and soak" while making little if any contribution. Each member should be encouraged to become a minister. Leaders should do everything possible to help people discover their God-given talents and then help them take an active part in the ministry. This is what I refer to as design-based ministry.

The design process involves leading each person who desires to serve the ministry through a ministry assessment program. Once they know how God has designed them with spiritual and natural gifts, passions, and temperament, the next step is ministry placement. This involves placing people in positions within or outside the ministry that best utilize their gifts, talents, and abilities.

▼▼▼

*Individual ministry leaders need to
school the new people about their departmental mission
and how their particular ministry contributes
to the mission as a whole.*

▲▲▲

Once assigned, those who lead these ministries will need to train the new people. This could involve lectures, manuals, video and audio tapes, and an internship or apprentice program. A vital part of this training is the propagation of the mission. Individual ministry leaders need to school the new people about their departmental mission and how their particular ministry contributes to the mission as a whole. First, the trainer shows the trainee how his or her ministry contributes to the departmental mission. Then, the trainer shows how the departmental mission fits with and aids in accomplishing the overall core organizational mission. The emphasis on mission is also included in the other training people receive once they're serving in their ministry niches.

6. EVALUATING

First Corinthians 3:13 says that someday God will judge the quality of every Christian's work by fire. Judgment involves evaluation. This evaluation takes place at the end of one's life. However, evaluation can be most helpful as one progresses through life in general and ministry in particular.

▼▼▼

What gets evaluated gets done.

▲▲▲

There is an age old maxim that says: "What gets evaluated gets done." Those who serve in any capacity in a ministry should receive regular evaluation along the way. While a little frightening at first, evaluation is a key ingredient to improvement. The ministries that God is blessing, regularly evaluate their people. A key question in evaluation is, Regardless of how well we've done what we've done, how can we do it better the next time? Not only will people improve at what they do, but change will emerge at the grassroots level. The results of evaluation can also mean promotions and awards as well as improvement and increased effectiveness.

7. CHALLENGING

What do we do with those who slip through the ministry "cracks"? These are people who are a part of the church or parachurch ministry who don't agree with the mission or values. They may have been a part of the ministry before the mission was established, or they may have been accepted because they thought they agreed with the ministry basics, its values and mission, only to discover later that they disagree.

▼▼▼

Scripture is replete with examples of leaders who challenged their people.

▲▲▲

Scripture is replete with examples of leaders who challenged their people. The prophets Jeremiah and Isaiah regularly challenged Israel to faithfulness to God. Jesus challenged all kinds of people to consider the truth of Scripture about him and about their own human condition. Paul challenged the churches such as Ephesus and Philippi to greater service for the Savior. In 2 Corinthians 13:5, he writes: "Examine yourselves to see whether you are in the faith; test yourselves."

In situations where people disagree with or are lukewarm toward the basics, the leadership is responsible to challenge them. This will alert all to the importance of the ministry's values and mission to the organization as a whole. It will serve to heighten the awareness of the mission to those who differ with it and challenge them to embrace it or move on to another ministry that's compatible with their mission.

8. PROMOTING

Most ministry organizations promote within. There is a trend among a growing number of churches, especially the megachurches, not to look to the seminaries for professional staff but to promote the qualified, gifted lay people who already lead and serve within the church. They may believe that seminarians are too academic and lack the vital leadership and people skills that are so vital to ministry. Parachurch ministries may operate in the same way. Many work with and train lay people such as college students, women, and international students. Those lay persons who prove exceptional are invited to join the staff of many of these ministries.

These organizations can use promotion to protect their core missions and values. One vital qualification for advancement is precise agreement on the mission and values of the ministry. The concept is simple: Those who agree are promoted, and those who don't agree aren't. The ministry has no choice in this matter. To promote people who don't agree with the ministry's mission, vision, and values is to compromise them and guarantee a fundamental, essential change in them over time.

9. REWARDING

Scripture clearly teaches that rewards are a legitimate way to encourage the faithful. Those who accept Christ and serve him in this life will be rewarded. In 1 Corinthians 3:10–15, Paul teaches that there will be a time in the future when Christ will return and judge all Christians according to the quality of their works. While all will spend eternity with him in heaven, not all will be rewarded equally (verses 14–15).

▼▼▼

What we learn from Scripture is that it's okay to reward those who faithfully serve our ministries.

▲▲▲

What we learn from Scripture is that it's okay to reward those who faithfully serve our ministries. And what we reward clearly communicates "what's important around here." Those who commit to the ministry's mission should be the happiest, most rewarded people in the ministry. These rewards are both formal and informal. Formal rewards are promotions, raises, wall plaques, trips, cash rewards, and so on. (Some might object to cash rewards, and this is understandable after all the scandal among the televangelists. However, who has ever been paid enough for what they do? Scripture says that "the worker deserves his wages" [1 Tim. 5:18].) Informal rewards are constant praise, either verbal or in writing; using the person as a positive example in illustrations; a smile, and many others.

SUMMARY

Nine Ways to Preserve Your Mission
Propagating
Recruiting
Enfolding
Inculturating
Training
Evaluating
Challenging
Promoting
Rewarding

QUESTIONS FOR THOUGHT AND DISCUSSION

1. What are some of the conflicts that your ministry has faced in the last year or two? Have you ever been a part of a ministry where there was no conflict? Do you believe that this is even possible? Why or why not?

2. How does your ministry handle conflict when it happens? If your ministry has a board, does it attempt to keep everybody happy no matter the cost? Does your ministry respond to conflict with compromise or consensus? Why?

3. How would you define ministry success? According to your definition, is your ministry successful? Why or why not? If yes, when should you prepare for a possible decline? What should you be doing at the present to prepare for a decline in your ministry?

4. If you are the leader or one of the leaders of your ministry, does your life incarnate and thus propagate the mission? Why or why not? Ask this question of someone else in the ministry and invite them to be candid. In what other ways does your ministry propagate its mission? What are some of the ways that you can improve at communicating your mission?

5. How do you recruit people for your ministry? Does your recruitment process preserve the mission? If yes, how? If no, why not? How are people enfolded into your ministry? Must they agree with the mission statement to be a part of your ministry? Why or why not?

6. Do you inculturate the people who join your ministry? If yes, how? If no, why not? Does the inculturating process attempt to preserve the ministry mission? Do you provide some form of training for those in your ministry? If yes, does it include mission preservation? If no, why not?

7. Does your ministry evaluate the performance of its people? If yes, how? If no, why not? Does the evaluation include agreement with the mission? Does your ministry challenge those who differ with its mission and values? If yes, how? If no, why not?

8. Does your ministry reward those who agree with and advance the ministry's mission statement? If no, why not? If yes, how, and has this preserved the mission? Does your organization promote those who agree with and work hard at accomplishing the mission? If yes, how? If no, why not? What are some other ways in which you might promote people who are loyal to and uphold the mission?

Appendix A
The Mission Audit

1. According to the Scriptures or the founding mission, what is this ministry supposed to be doing?

2. What is it really doing?

3. If your answers to 1 and 2 are different, then how do you explain the discrepancy?

4. If the ministry ship continues on its present course, where will it dock in the next few years? Is this good or bad?

5. Do your key leaders know where the ministry is going? Do all agree on that direction?

6. Assuming the ministry is off course, what would it take for it to change course and begin doing what it's supposed to be doing?

7. Do you believe this will happen? Why or why not? If so, when?

8. Are you and all key leaders willing to do whatever it takes to move in a different direction? If not, why?

Appendix B
How to Develop Your Mission Statement

Step 1: What are we supposed to be doing according to the Bible?
- What kind of ministry are you involved in?
- Whom are you trying to serve?
- How will your ministry serve people?

Step 2: Can you articulate your mission in a written statement?
- What words communicate best with your target group?
- Do your people understand what you've written?
- Does your format convey well your mission?

Step 3: Is the mission statement brief and simple?
- Have you committed information overload?
- Does your statement pass the "T-shirt test"?
- Can you express your mission in one sentence?
- Is your mission memorable?

Step 4: Is your mission statement broad but clear?
- Is your statement broad enough?
- Is your statement clear?
- Does your statement pass the "people-test"?

Index

Aubrey Malphurs is the president of Vision Ministries International and is available for consultation and training on various topics related to leadership, values, mission, vision, strategy, church planting, church renewal, etc. Those wishing to contact him for consulting or speaking engagements may do so through:

Vision Ministries International
3909 Swiss Avenue
Dallas, TX 75204
1-214-841-3777

STRATEGY 2000

Churches Making Disciples for the Next Millennium
Aubrey Malphurs

What does a disciple-making church look like? Experienced pastor and church planter Aubrey Malphurs shows how strategy plays a vital role in churches becoming disciple-makers, not just decision-makers. He examines the preparation, the process, and the product of a strategy. This practical guide offers step-by-step planning techniques for the local church and parachurch ministry along with sample strategies.

0-8254-3196-4   240 pp.

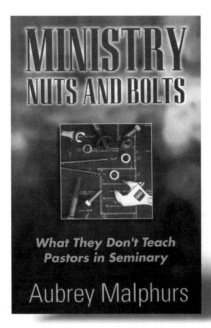

MINISTRY NUTS AND BOLTS

What They Don't Teach Pastors in Seminary
Aubrey Malphurs

Most seminary graduates think ministry is 95 percent preaching. But "preaching alone will not get the job done," says Malphurs in the introduction. Why not? Because the four things that drive an effective ministry are values, mission, vision, and strategy. Using over twenty-five charts and figures, Malphurs demonstrates how to implement these essential concepts into a local church ministry.

0-8254-3190-5   192 pp.

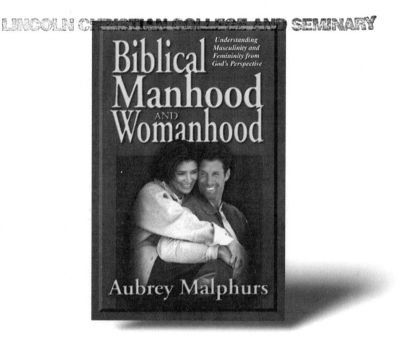

BIBLICAL MANHOOD AND WOMANHOOD
Understanding Masculinity and Femininity from God's Perspective
Aubrey Malphurs

Randy grew up in a dysfunctional home, the son of an alcoholic father and emotionally detached mother. Carol grew up in a single-parent home where she decided early in life to control her own life and protect herself against the pain of losing her father in a divorce. Randy and Carol eventually attend the same church, become Christians, and later marry. How are they to understand the Bible's teaching on what it means to be a man and a woman related to one another as God intended?

The questions and struggles of these two composite characters, typical of the baby boom and baby bust generations all across America, form the basis for this new work that affirms the biblical plan for the marriage partnership.

0-8254-3195-6   160 pp.